The Book of God

In the Light of the Higher Criticism

G. W. Foote

The Book of God: In the Light of the Higher Criticism

Copyright © 2020 Bibliotech Press
All rights reserved

ISBN: 978-1-64799-189-0

CONTENTS

CONTENTS

I. INTRODUCTION

During the fierce controversy between the divines of the Protestant Reformation and those of the Roman Catholic Church, the latter asserted that the former treated the Bible—and treated it quite naturally—as a wax nose, which could be twisted into any shape and direction. Those who championed the living voice of God in the Church, against the dead letter of the written Bible, were always prone to deride the consequences of private judgment when applied to such a large and heterogeneous volume as the Christian Scriptures. They contended that the Bible is a misleading book when read by itself in the mere light of human reason; that any doctrine may be proved from it by a judicious selection of texts; and that Christianity would break up into innumerable sects unless the Church acted as the inspired interpreter of the inspired revelation. They argued, further, that the Bible was really not what the Protestants supposed it to be; and what they said on this point was a curious anticipation of a good deal of the so-called Higher Criticism.

Both sides were right, and both sides were wrong, in this dispute. The Protestants were right against the Church; the Catholics were right against the Bible. It was reserved for Rationalism to accept and harmonise the double truth, and to wage war against both infallibilities.

The Bible is said to be inspired, but the man who reads it is not. The consequence is that he deduces from it a creed in harmony with his own taste, temper, fancy, and intelligence. He lays emphasis on what fits in with this creed, and slurs over all that is opposed to it. Every one of the various and conflicting Protestant sects is founded upon one and the same infallible book. "The Bible teaches this," says one; "The Bible teaches that," says another. And they are both right. The Bible does teach the doctrines of all the sects. But do they not

1

contradict each other? They do. What is the explanation, then? Why this—the Bible contradicts itself.

The self-contradictions of the Bible have occasioned the writing of many "Harmonies," in which it is sought to be proved that all the apparent discrepancies are most admirable agreements when they are properly understood. All that is requisite is to add a word here, and subtract a word there; to regard one and the same word as having several different meanings, and several different words as having one and the same meaning; and, above all things, to apply this method with a strong and earnest desire to find harmony everywhere, and a pious intention of giving the Bible the benefit of the doubt in every case of perplexity.

This sort of jugglery, which would be derided and despised in the case of any other book, is now falling into discredit. Most of the clergy are ashamed of it. They frankly own, since it can no longer be denied, that a more honest art of criticism is necessary to save the Bible from general contempt.

But the "Harmony" game is not the only one that is played out. All the "Reconciliations" of the Bible with science, history, morality, and common sense, are sharing the same fate. The higher clergy leave such exhibitions of perverted ingenuity to laymen like the late Mr. Gladstone. Divines like Canon Driver see that this mental tight-rope dancing may cause astonishment, but will never produce conviction. They therefore recognise the difficulties, and seek for a more subtle and plausible method of removing them. They admit that Moses and Darwin are at variance with each other; that a great deal of Bible "history" is legendary, and some of it distinctly false; that such stories as those of Lot's wife and Jonah's whale are decidedly incredible; that some passages of Scripture are vulgar and brutal, and others detestably inhuman; and that it is positively useless to disguise the fact. Yet they are naturally anxious to keep the Bible on its old pedestal; and this can only be done by means of a new theory of inspiration. Accordingly, these gentlemen tell us that the Bible is not the Word of God, but it contains the Word of

2

God. Its writers were inspired, but their own natural faculties were not entirely suppressed by the divine spirit. Sometimes the writer's spirit was predominant in the combination, and the composition was mainly that of an unregenerate son of Adam. At other times the divine spirit was predominant, and the result was lofty religion and pure ethics. Moreover, the sacred writers were only inspired in one direction. God gave them a lift, as it were, in spiritual matters; but in science and sociology he let them blunder along as they could.

The old wax nose is now receiving a decided new twist, and a considerable number of accomplished and clever divines are engaged in manipulating it. One of them is Dean Farrar, who has recently published a bulky volume on *The Bible: its Meaning and Supremacy*, which we shall subject to a very careful criticism.

Dean Farrar's book contains nothing that is new to fairly well-read sceptics. It presents the commonplaces of modern Biblical criticism, with a due regard to the interests of "the grand old book" and of "true" and "fundamental" Christianity, which is probably no more than the particular form of Christianity that is likely to weather the present storm of controversy. But although this book contains no startling novelties, it is of importance as the work of a dignitary of the Church of England. It is also of value, inasmuch as it will be read by many persons who would shrink from Strauss and Thomas Paine. It is well that someone should tell Christians the truth, if not the *whole* truth, about the Bible, and tell it them from within the fold of faith. His motive in doing so may be less a regard for truth itself than for the immediate interests of his own Church; but the main thing is that he does it, and Freethinkers may be glad even if they are not grateful.

Dr. Farrar's book has an Introduction, and we propose to examine it first. He opens by telling the clergy that they ought not to pursue an "ostrich policy" in regard to religious difficulties; that they should not indulge in "vituperative phrases," nor assume a "disdainful infallibility"; that they do wrong in denouncing as "wicked," "blasphemous," or "dangerous" every conviction which

3

differs from their own form of orthodoxy; and that they must not expect all that they choose to assert to be "accepted with humble acquiescence." No doubt this advice is quite necessary; and the fact that it is so shows the value of Christianity, after eighteen centuries of trial, as a training-school in the virtues of modesty and humility, to say nothing of justice and temperance.

The clergy are also invited by Dr. Farrar to recognise the general diffusion of scepticism:—

"In recent years much has been written under the assumption that Christianity no longer deserves the dignity of a refutation; or that, at any rate, the bases on which it rests have been seriously undermined. The writings of freethinkers are widely disseminated among the working classes. The Church of Christ has lost its hold on multitudes of men in our great cities. Those of the clergy who are working in the crowded centres of English life can hardly be unaware of the extent to which scepticism exists among our artizans. Many of them have been persuaded to believe that the Church is a hostile and organised hypocrisy."

This is a sad state of things, and how is it to be met?

Not by denouncing reason as a wild beast, nor yet by relying on emotion and ceremonial, for "no religious system will be permanent which is not based on the convictions of the intellect." Dr. Farrar recommends a different policy. He has "frequently observed that the objections urged against Christianity are aimed at dogmas which are no part of Christian faith, or are in no wise essential to its integrity." Even men of science have been led astray by objections "based on travesties of its real tenets." One of these false opinions is that "which maintains the supposed inerrancy and supernatural infallibility of every book, sentence, and word of the Holy Bible." This is the principal point to be dealt with; it is here that we must make an adjustment. Nine-tenths of the case of sceptics "is made up of attacks on the Bible," and the only way to answer them is to show that they misunderstand it, and that what they demolish is not

4

Christianity, but "a mummy elaborately painted in its semblance," or "a scarecrow set up in its guise."

"It is no part of the Christian faith," Dr. Farrar says, "to maintain that every word of the Bible was dictated supernaturally, or is equally valuable, or free from all error, or on the loftiest levels of morality, as finally revealed." Such a view of the Bible has been popularly expressed by divines, but they really did not mean it, and it "never formed any part of the Catholic creed of Christendom." The doctrine of everlasting punishment is another of these delusions. There is such a thing as future punishment, but it is not everlasting—it is only eternal. In the same way, the Bible is the Word of God, but it is not infallible—it is only inspired. And what *that* means we shall see as we proceed.

II. THE BIBLE CANON

The first chapter of Dean Farrar's book deals with the Bible Canon. After another slap at the poor benighted Christians who still hold that every word of Scripture is "supernaturally dictated and infallibly true," Dr. Farrar remarks that the Bible is "not a single nor even a homogeneous book." Strictly speaking, it is not a book, but a library; and, as is pointed out later on, it is the remains of a much larger collection which has mostly perished. The Canon of the Old Testament was "arrived at by slow and uncertain degrees." The common assertion, that it was fixed by Ezra and the so-called Great Synagogue in the fifth century before Christ, is in direct opposition to the facts. It was not really *settled* until seventy years after the birth of Christ, when the Rabbis met at Jamnia, and decided in favor of our present thirty-nine books. According to Dr. Farrar, there was no special influence from heaven in the determination of the Canon. It was a work which God left to "the *ordinary* influences of the Holy Ghost." Let us see then how these influences operated on the last and most critical occasion. "The gathering at Jamnia," says Dr. Farrar, "was a tumultuous assemblage, and in the faction fights of the Rabbinic parties blood was shed by their scholars. Hence the decision was regarded as irrevocable and sealed by blood." Such are the *ordinary* influences of the Holy Ghost. Its *extraordinary* influences may be easily imagined. Their history is written in blood and fire in every country in Christendom.

Dr. Farrar allows that the Canon of the New Testament was formed "in the same gradual and tentative way." Many Gospels, Epistles, and Apocalypses were "current" in the "first two centuries." Some of them were "quoted as sacred books" and read aloud in Christian churches. Seven, at least, of the books which are now canonical were then "disputed"—namely, the Second Epistle of

6

St. Peter, the Second and Third Epistles of St. John, the Epistle to the Hebrews, the Epistles of St. James and St. Jude, and the Book of Revelation. The Canon was "formally and officially settled" by the Council of Laodicea (a.d. 363), and the two Councils of Carthage (a.d. 397 and 419), the decrees of which were sanctioned by the Trullian Council (a.d. 692), nearly seven hundred years after Christ. Dr. Farrar holds, however, that these Councils merely registered the general agreement of the Christian Church. The real test of canonicity is not the decision of Councils, which may and do err, but "the verifying faculty of the Christian consciousness." Dr. Farrar's argument, if it means anything at all, implies that while Councils may err, consisting as they do of fallible men, this "Christian consciousness" is really infallible. But as this Christian consciousness only exists, after all, in individual Christians, however numerous they may be, or through however many centuries they may be continued, it is difficult to see how the greatest multitude of fallibilities can make up one infallibility. And unless it can, it is also difficult to see how Dr. Farrar can have an infallible Canon. He disclaims the authority of the Church, on which Catholics rely; indeed, he says it can hardly be said that the "whole Church" has pronounced any opinion on the Canon at all. What really happened is perhaps unconsciously admitted by Dr. Farrar in a rather simple footnote. "Books were judged," he says, "by the congruity of their contents with the general Christian conviction." Precisely so; the books did not decide the doctrine, but the doctrine decided the fate of the books. And how was the doctrine decided? By fierce controversy, by forgery and sophistication, by partisan struggles, and finally, after the adhesion of Constantine, by faction fights that involved the loss of myriads (some say millions) of lives.

Not the slightest attempt is made by Dr. Farrar to meet the difficulty of his position; indeed, he seems unaware that the difficulty exists. All he sees is the difficulty of the positions taken up by the Catholics and the early Protestants. It never occurs to him that he has only shifted from one difficulty to another. The

7

Catholics rely upon the living voice of God in the Church. That covers everything, like the sky; and is perfectly satisfactory, if you can only accept it. The early Protestants repudiated the authority of the Church, at least as represented by the Pope and Councils; but they acknowledged the authority of the *primitive* Church. They were shrewd enough to see that what cannot possibly rest on mere reason must rest somewhere on authority; so they admitted as much as was sufficient to cover the Scriptures and the Creeds, and refused to go a step farther. Dr. Farrar breaks away from both parties, and what is the result? He talks about the Canon of the New Testament being formed "by the exercise of enlightened reason," but he lays down no criterion by which reason can decide whether a book is inspired or not, or so specially inspired as to require a place in the Canon. The "verifying faculty of the Christian consciousness" is one of those comfortable phrases, like the blessed word Mesopotamia, which are designed to save the pains of accuracy and the trouble of definite thought. What light does it really shed upon the following questions? Why is the Protestant Canon different from the Catholic Canon? Is it owing to some inexplicable difference in the "verifying faculty of the Christian consciousness" in the two cases; and by what test shall we decide when the Christian consciousness delivers two contradictory verdicts? Why is the book of Ecclesiastes in the Canon, while the book of Ecclesiasticus is (by the Protestants) relegated to the Apocrypha? Why is the book of Esther in the Canon, and the book of Judith in the Apocrypha? Why is the book of Jonah in the Canon, and the book of Tobit in the Apocrypha? Why is the book of Proverbs in the Canon, and the book of the Wisdom of Solomon in the Apocrypha? These are questions which the early Protestants answered in their way, but we defy Dr. Farrar to answer them at all.

Let us follow Dr. Farrar into his second chapter. He states, truly enough, that both the Old and the New Testaments represent "the selected and fragmentary remains of an extensive literature." Many books referred to in the Old Testament are lost. Some of the canonical books are anonymous; we do not know who wrote them.

Others bear the names of men "by whom they could not have been composed." The Pentateuch is "a work of composite structure," which has been "edited and re-edited several times." The Psalms are a collection of sacred poems in "five separate books of very various antiquity." The Proverbs consist of "four or five different collections." The New Testament is a selection from the voluminous Christian literature of the earliest centuries. Many Gospels were already in existence when St. Luke prepared his own. "It is all but certain," Dr. Farrar says, "that St. Paul, and probable that the other Apostles, must have written many letters which are no longer preserved." That is to say, some letters actually written by St. Paul were allowed to perish, while others not written by him were allowed to bear his name, and were placed as his in the New Testament Canon! There are passages in the Gospels that are known to be interpolations; for instance, the story of the Woman taken in Adultery. This story is "exquisite and supremely valuable," but it is bracketed in the Revised Version as of "doubtful genuineness." Such passages are eliminated because they do not "meet the standard of modern critical requirements." *O sancta simplicitas!* Is there any reason, in the natural sense of that word, for believing that John the Apostle wrote the rest of the Fourth Gospel, any more than he wrote this rejected story? Dr. Farrar strains at gnats and swallows camels, and prides himself on his discrimination.

His references to Justin Martyr and Papias seem less than ingenuous. It is not true that Justin Martyr "freely uses the Gospels." Dr. Farrar admits that he "does not name them." Saying that he "used" them is quietly assuming that they existed. All that Justin Martyr does, as a matter of fact, is to cite sayings ascribed to Jesus, but not in one single case does he cite a saying of Jesus in exactly the form in which it appears in the Four Gospels. Supposing that he wrote freely, and had ever so bad a memory, and never took the trouble to refer to the originals, it is simply inconceivable that he should never be right. Now and then he must have deviated into accuracy. And the fact that he never does is plain proof that he had

9

not our Gospels before him. Nor does Papias mention "the Gospels." He mentions only two, Matthew and Mark, and he says that Matthew was written in *Hebrew*. Now, the earliest date at which Papias can be fixed is a.d. 140. This is chosen by Dr. Farrar, and we will let it pass unchallenged. And what follows? Why this, that no Christian writer before a.d. 140 betrays that he has so much as heard of *any* Gospel, and even then but *two* are known instead of *four*, and one of these is most certainly *not* the Gospel which opens the New Testament.

All this was proved a quarter of a century ago by the author of *Supernatural Religion*—a work which is systematically ignored by the so-called Higher Critics because its author was a pronounced Rationalist. An excellent summary of this writer's demonstrations appears in the late Matthew Arnold's *God and the Bible*:—

"He seems to have looked out and brought together, to the best of his powers, every extant *passage* in which, between the year 70 and the year 170 of our era, a writer might be supposed to be quoting one of our Four Gospels.

"And it turns out that there is constantly the same sort of variation from our Gospels, a variation inexplicable in men quoting from a real Canon, and quite unlike what is found in men quoting from our Four Gospels later on. It may be said that the Old Testament, too, is often quoted loosely. True; but it is also quoted exactly; and long passages of it are thus quoted. It would be nothing that our canonical Gospels were often quoted loosely, if long passages from them, or if passages, say, of even two or three verses, were sometimes quoted exactly. But from writers before Irenæus not one such passage can be produced so quoted. And the author of *Supernatural Religion* by bringing all the alleged quotations forward, has proved it." [1]

Now what is the exact value of these demonstrations? We will give it in Mr. Arnold's words: "There is no evidence of the

---

[1] Arnold, God and the Bible, pp. 222-3.

establishment of our Four Gospels as a Gospel-Canon, or even of their existence as they now finally stand at all, before the last quarter of the second century." Not only is there no evidence of the orthodox theory, but, as Mr. Arnold says, the "great weight of evidence is against it."

Dr. Giles—another ignored writer, although a clergyman of the Church of England—had said and proved the very same thing in his *Christian Records*; and had appended the following significant declaration:—

"There is positive proof, in the writings of the first ages of Christianity, that the same question as to the age and authorship of the books of the New Testament was even then agitated, and if it was then set at rest, this was done, not by a deliberate sentence of the judge, but by burning all the evidence on which one side of the controversy was supported," [2]

It is probable that Dr. Farrar is well aware that our Four Gospels cannot be traced beyond the second half of the second century—that is, considerably more than a century after the alleged date of the death of Christ. But he shrinks from a frank admission of the fact, and leaves the reader to find it out for himself.

Instead of making this important and, as some think, damning admission, Dr. Farrar continues his remarks on the Bible Canon. That thirty-six books are accepted "on the authority of the Church" simply means, he tells us, that they are accepted "by the general consensus of Christians." The whole Church, as such, has hardly pronounced an opinion on the subject. The Churchmen who voted at Laodicea and Carthage "exercised no independent judgment," and their critical knowledge was "elementary." Nor was the decision of the Council of Trent any real improvement. Dr. Farrar approves the reply of the Reformed Churches, that "any man may reject books claiming to be Holy Scripture if he do not feel the evidence of their contents." But this is to make every man a judge,

---

[2] Dr. Giles, Christian Records, p. 10.

11

not only of what the Bible means, but also of what it should contain. Each unfettered Christian may therefore make up a Bible for himself; which is simply chaos come again. What then is the way of escape from this grotesque confusion? Dr. Farrar indicates it with a crooked finger:—

"The decision as to what books are or are not to be regarded as true Scripture, though we believe it to be wise and right, depends on no infallible decision. It must satisfy the scientific and critical as well as the spiritual requirements of each age."

This reduces the Bible Canon to a perpetual transformation scene. It is a tacit confession that the Protestant Bible is an arbitrary collection of questionable documents; that it has nothing to plead for itself but common usage; that its very contents, as well as their interpretation, are liable to change; in short, that if the Catholic stands upon the rock of implicit faith, and defies all dangers by closing his eyes and clutching the reassuring hand of his Holy Mother Church, the Protestant flounders about with the poor little dark-lantern of private judgment in a frightful mud-ocean—his old rock of faith in an infallible Bible having been reduced to dust by the engines of criticism, and finally to slush by a downflow from the lofty reservoir of pure reason. [3]

_____

[3] It would be a pity to omit an amusing instance of the contemptuous dogmatism of Christian divines when they had the field to themselves. Dr. William Whitaker, a famous learned writer on the side of the Reformation in England, in his Disputation with two of the foremost Jesuits, Bellarmine and Stapleton, wrote as follows:—"Jerome, in the Proem of his Commentaries on Daniel, relates that Porphyry the philosopher wrote a volume against the book of our prophet Daniel, and affirmed that what is now extant under the name of Daniel was not published by the ancient prophet, but by some later Daniel, who lived in the times of Antiochus Epiphanes. But we need not regard what the impious Porphyry may have written, who mocked at all the scriptures and religion itself." Well, this opinion of the blasphemous Porphyry, whose writings were burnt by the Christian Church, is now accepted by the Higher Critics. Canon Driver, for instance, admits that the Book of Daniel is not the work of Daniel, that it could not have been written earlier than 300 B.C., and that "it is at least probable that it was composed under the persecution of Antiochus Epiphanes, B.C. 168 or 167"

III. THE BIBLE AND SCIENCE

Having examined Dean Farrar's observations on the Bible Canon, and seen that it is a more or less arbitrary selection from Hebrew and early Christian literature, many of the books being anonymous, while others bear the names of authors who did not write them, and most of them being much later compositions than orthodoxy supposes; we now take a leap forward to his twelfth chapter to see what he has to say on the subject of the Bible and Science. His first object is to drive home to his co-religionists the mischief of adhering to the old doctrine of Bible infallibility. Consequently he does not mince matters in dealing with the difficulties of the literal theory of inspiration. Writers like Gaussen contend that the Bible is a perfect authority in matters of science. Mr. Gladstone argues that Moses supernaturally anticipated the teachings of modern evolution, and that the inspired fishermen of Galilee, notably St. Peter, no less supernaturally anticipated all that modern astronomy teaches as to the final destiny of our planet. Dr. Farrar declines to follow them in this perilous path. He does not walk in the opposite direction, for that would lead him among the "infidels." He strikes off at right angles, and takes the line that the Bible was never intended to teach science, or anything else but religion. He quotes with approval the saying of Archbishop Sumner, that "the Scriptures have never revealed a scientific truth." He maintains that the writers of Scripture had only a natural knowledge of exact science; and that was precious little, and was indeed rather ignorance than knowledge, as they belonged to "the most unscientific of all nations in the most unscientific of all ages." "It is now understood by competent inquirers," he says, "that geology is

---

(Introduction to the Literature of the Old Testament, p. 467). This involves that the fulfilled prophecies of Daniel were written after the events.

13

God's revelation to us of one set of truths, and Genesis of quite another." "Nature," he says, "is a book which contains a revelation of God in one sphere, and Scripture a book which contains a revelation of him in another. Both books have often been misread, but no *truth* revealed in the one can be irreconcilable with any truth revealed in the other." This, however, is a mere truism; for one truth cannot be irreconcilable with another truth. Dr. Farrar's statement sounds imposing and consolatory, but when you look into its meaning you see it is only a pulpit platitude.

But before we proceed to criticise Dr. Farrar's position, let us glance at his attack upon the literalists. He charges them with having opposed and persecuted every modern science, and with having manufactured the most absurd scientific theories from the text of the Bible; the said theories being not only ludicrous, but irreconcilably opposed to each other. Lactantius, with the Bible in his hand, ridiculed the rotundity of the earth. Roger Bacon and Galileo were imprisoned and tortured for teaching true science instead of the false science of the Church. John Wesley declared the Copernican astronomy to be in opposition to Scripture. Thomas Burnet's "Sacred Theory of the Earth," founded upon the Bible, was assailed by William Whiston, who based a different "Sacred Theory" upon the very same book. Buffon, the great French scientist, was compelled by the Sorbonne to recant, and to abandon everything in his writings that was "contrary to the narrative of Moses." Even when God (that is to say Dr. Simpson) gave to the world the priceless boon of anaesthetics, there were many Biblicists who declared that the use of chloroform in cases of painful confinement was flying in the face of God's curse upon the daughters of Eve. Catholic and Protestant have alike pitted the Bible against Science, and both have been ignominiously beaten.

But this is not all. The theologians have been disgraced as well as defeated. With respect to the Buffon case, for instance, Dr. Farrar writes as follows:—

"The line now taken by apologists is very different from that of

14

previous centuries, and less honest. It declares that Genesis and geology are in exact accord. It no longer refuses to believe the facts of nature, but instead of this it boldly sophisticates the facts of Scripture."

John Stuart Mill said that every new truth passes through three phases of reception. At first, it is declared to be false and dangerous; secondly, it is discovered that there is something to be said for it; lastly, its opponents turn round and declare "we said so all along." Dr. Farrar dots all the "i's" in Mill's statement. He asserts that "religious teachers" first say of every scientific discovery, "It is blasphemous and contrary to Scripture." Next they say, "There is nothing in Scripture which absolutely contradicts it." Finally they say, "It is distinctly revealed in Scripture itself."

Dr. Farrar puts the historic case against "orthodoxy"—which, of course, is not Christianity!—in the following fashion:—

"The history of most modern sciences has been as follows. Its discoverers have been proscribed, anathematised, and, in every possible instance, silenced or persecuted; yet before a generation has passed the champions of a spurious orthodoxy have had to confess that their interpretations were erroneous; and—for the most part without an apology and without a blush—have complacently invented some new line of exposition by which the phrases of Scripture can be squared into semblable accordance with the now acknowledged facts."

Even in the comparatively recent case of Darwin this was perfectly true. Dr. Farrar, who preached Darwin's funeral sermon in Westminster Abbey, says that he "endured the fury of pulpits and Church Congresses." He did so with quiet dignity; not an angry word escaped him. Yet before Darwin's death not only was the scientific world converted, but leading theologians said that, if Darwinism were proved to be true, there was "nothing in it contrary to the creeds of the Catholic faith."

Darwin never answered the clergy. He had better work to do. All he did was to smile at them. In one of his letters he said that when

15

the men of science are agreed about anything all the clergy have to do is to say ditto. He understood that when science is victorious it will always have clerical patronage. Had he been able to do it, he would have smiled, in that beautiful benevolent way of his, at Dr. Farrar's funeral sermon. The worthy Dean thought they had got Darwin at last; and the grand old philosopher might have said, "Why yes, my *corpse!*"

So much for Dr. Farrar's impeachment of "orthodoxy" and its doctrine of plenary inspiration. Let us now examine his own position, and see whether it is logical as well as convenient.

Take the first chapter of Genesis. It is not a scientific revelation, though it seems to be. Whoever wrote it had only the science of his time. Nevertheless, it is of "transcendent value," according to Dr. Farrar. "Its true and deep object," he says, "was to set right an erring world in the supremely important knowledge that there was one God and Father of us all, the Creator of heaven and earth, a God who saw all things which he has made, and pronounced them to be very good."

This is very pretty in its way; but how absurd it is in the light of the fact that the Hebrew creation story is all *borrowed!* While the Jews were desert nomads, long before the concoction of their sacred scriptures the doctrine of a Creator of heaven and earth was known in India and in Egypt, not to recite a list of other nations. If this is all the first chapter of Genesis teaches, we may well exclaim, "Thank you for nothing!" It is a curious "revelation" which only discloses what is familiar. Had the Bible never been written, had the Jews never existed, the "true and deep object" of the first chapter of Genesis would have been quite as well subserved. Wherever the Christian missionaries have gone they have found the creation story in front of them. Wherever they took it they were carrying coals to Newcastle.

We venture to suggest that if Dr. Farrar thinks that all things God has made are very good, there are many persons who do not share his opinion. It would be idle to read that text to a sailor pursued by

16

a shark. We could multiply this instance a thousandfold; but why give a list of all the predatory and parasitical creatures on this planet, from human tyrants and despoilers down to cholera microbes? Dr. Farrar may reply that everything ends in mystery, that we must have faith, that it is our interest as well as our duty to believe. But that is exactly what the Catholic Church says, and Dr. Farrar laughs it to scorn. The truth is, that all theology is ultimately a matter of faith; and the quarrel about more or less is a domestic difference. The greater difference is between Faith and Reason. This was clearly seen by Cardinal Newman, who pointed out that every mystery of the Roman Catholic faith is matched by a mystery in Protestant theology.

Finally, we have to remark that Dr. Farrar overlooks a very important point in this controversy. Having argued that the Bible was not intended to teach science, and has not in fact helped the world to a single scientific discovery; having also admitted that the Bible has all along been used to hinder the progress of natural knowledge, and to justify the persecution of honest investigators; he seems to imagine that there is no more to be said. But there is *much* more to be said. We forbear to press the objection that Omniscience was very curiously employed in entangling a religious revelation with scientific blunders, which would necessarily retard the progress of scientific truth, and therefore of human civilisation. What we wish to emphasise is less open to the retort that Omniscience is beyond our finite judgment. We desire to urge that the Bible is not simply non-scientific. It is anti-scientific. Let us take, for instance, the story of the creation and fall of man. Even if it be not taken literally, but allegorically, it is thoroughly antagonistic to the teachings of Evolution. At the very least it implies that man is something special and unique, whereas he is included in the general scheme of biology, and is but "the paragon of animals." Get rid of the actual garden and the actual tree of knowledge, as Dr. Farrar does, and there still remains the fact that the fall of man is a falsehood, and the ascent of man a verity. The allegory does not correspond to the essential truth of man's history; and in spite of all

17

the flattering rhetoric with which Dr. Farrar invests it—a rhetoric so inharmonious with its own consummate simplicity—there is something inexpressibly childish to the modern mind in the awful heinousness which is attributed to the mere eating of forbidden fruit. An act is really not vicious because it is prohibited, or virtuous because it conforms to the dictates of authority. When man attains to intellectual maturity he smiles at the ethical trick which was played upon his youthful ignorance. It is not sufficient to tell him that he must do this, and must not do that. He requires a reason. His intelligence must go hand in hand with his emotions. It is this union, indeed, which constitutes what we call conscience.

The truth is that the Bible is steeped in superstition and supernaturalism. Its cosmogony, its conception of man's origin and position in the universe, its infantile legends, its miracles and magic, its theory of madness and disease, its doctrine of the external efficacy of prayer, its idea that man's words and wishes avail to change the sweep of universal forces and the operation of their immutable laws: all this is in direct opposition to the letter and spirit of Science. The special pleading of clergymen like Dr. Farrar may afford a temporary relief to trembling Christians, and keep them for a further term in the fold of faith; but it will never make the slightest impression upon sceptics, unless it fills them with contemptuous pity for a number of clever men who are obliged, for personal reasons, to practise the lowest arts of sophistry.

IV. MIRACLES AND WITCHCRAFT

Dr. Farrar, as we have seen, holds that the Bible is not a revelation in science. The inspired writers were, in such matters, left to their natural knowledge. The Holy Spirit taught them that God made the world and all which it inhabits; but *how* it was made they only conjectured. The truth, in *this* respect, was left to the discovery of later ages.

This is a pretty and convenient theory, but it does not provide for every difficulty in the relationship between science and the Bible. There still remain the questions of miracles and witchcraft.

Dr. Farrar does not discuss these questions thoroughly. He only ventures a few observations. In his opinion, the two miracles of the Creation and the Incarnation "include the credibility of *all* other miracles." We agree with him. Admit creation out of nothing, and you need not be astonished at the transformation of water into wine. Admit the birth of a boy from a virgin mother, and you need not raise physiological objections to the story of a man being safely entertained for three days in a whale's intestines. It is absurd to strain at gnats after swallowing camels. For this reason we are unable to understand Dr. Farrar's fastidiousness. He is ready to believe that some miracles are mistaken metaphors, that some were due to the action of unnoticed or ill-understood natural causes, and that others were providential occurrences instead of supernatural events. All this, however, is but a concession to the sceptical spirit. It is throwing out the children to the wolves. It may stop their pursuit for a little while, but they will come on again, and flesh their jaws upon the parents.

A mixed criterion of true miracles is laid down by Dr. Farrar. They must be (1) adequately attested, and (2) wrought for adequate

19

ends, and (3) in accordance with the revealed laws of God's immediate dealings with man. The second and third conditions are too fanciful for discussion. They are, in fact, entirely subjective. The first condition is the only one which can be applied with decisive accuracy. The miracles must be *adequately attested*. But was it not David Hume who declared that "in all history" there is not a single miracle attested in this manner? And did not Professor Huxley say that Hume's assertion was "least likely" to be challenged by those who are used to weighing evidence and giving their decision with a due sense of moral responsibility?

It is easy enough to sneer at Hume. It is just as easy to answer what he never said. What the apologists of Christianity have to do is to take a single miracle of their faith and show that it rests upon adequate evidence. Anything short of this is intellectual thimble-rigging.

Dr. Farrar does not face this dreadful task. He treats us, instead, to some personal observations on the Fall, the Tower of Babel, Balaam's ass, Joshua's arrest of the sun and moon, and Jonah's submarine excursion. Let us examine these observations.

No Christian, says Dr. Farrar, is called upon to believe in an actual Garden of Eden and an actual talking serpent. Christians have believed in these things by the million. But that was before the clergy invented "the Higher Criticism" to disarm "infidelity." They know better now. The story of the Fall is false as a narrative. It is true as a "vivid pictorial representation of the origin and growth of sin in the human heart." All the literature of the world has failed to set forth anything "comparable to it in insight." Therefore it is "inspired."

How hollow this sounds when we recollect that the Hebrew story of the Fall was borrowed from the Persian mythology! How much hollower when we consider it as it stands, stripped of the veil of fancy and divested of the glamor of association! The "insight" of the inspired writer could only represent God as the landlord of an orchard, and man as a being with a taste for forbidden apples. The

20

"philosopheme," as Dr. Farrar grandiosely styles it, is so absurd in its native nakedness that Rabbis and other divines have suspected a carnal mystery behind the apples, in order to give the "sin" of Adam and Eve a darker vein of sensuality. [4]

Nor is this all. The very idea of a Fall is inconsistent with Evolution. The true Garden of Eden lies not behind us, but before us. The true Paradise is not the earth as God made it for man, but the earth as man is making it for himself. The Bible teaches the *descent* of man. Science teaches the *ascent* of man. And the two theories are the antipodes of each other, not only in physical history, but in every moral and spiritual implication.

With regard to the story of the tower of Babel, we must not regard it as an inspired account of the origin of the diversity of human language. That is what it appears to be upon the face of it. But philology has exploded this childish legend, and a new meaning must be read into it. According to Dr. Farrar, it is a "symbolic way of expressing the truth that God breaks up into separate nationalities the tyrannous organisation of cruel despotisms." Now we venture to say that there is not a suggestion of this in the text. And the "truth" which Dr. Farrar reads into it so arbitrarily is a phenomenon of modern times. Nationality is a great force at present, but in ancient days the only power that could bind tribes together in one polity was a military despotism. From the point of view of evolution, both conquest and slavery were inevitable steps in the progress of civilisation. It is really nothing against the ancient Jews, for instance, that they fought like devils and made slaves of their enemies. It was the fashion of the time. The mischief comes in when we are told that their proceedings were under the sanction and control of God.

Dr. Farrar next tackles the story of Balaam, which is "another theme for ignorant ridicule." It is astonishing how sublime these

---

[4] We cannot elaborate this point in a publication which is intended for general reading. Suffice it to say that one famous commentator suggests that Eve was seduced by an ape.

Bible wonders become in the light of the Higher Criticism. A talking ass sounds like an echo of the Arabian Nights. But the author himself never intended you to believe it. Dr. Farrar is quite sure of that. You must forget the ass, and fix your attention on Balaam. Then you perceive that the story is "rich in almost unrivalled elements of moral edification." That is to say, you perceive it if you borrow Dr. Farrar's spectacles. But if you look with your own naked eyes you see that ass in the foreground of the picture, with outstretched neck and open jaws, holding forth to an astonished universe.

With regard to Joshua's supreme miracle, Dr. Farrar avows his unbelief. A battle ode got mistaken for actual history. "He who chooses," says Dr. Farrar, "may believe that the most fundamental laws of the universe were arrested to enable Joshua to slaughter a few more hundred fugitives; and he who chooses may believe that nothing of the kind ever entered into the mind of the narrator." You pay your money and take your choice. Shape the old wax nose as you please. Believe what you like, and disbelieve what you like— and swear the author disbelieved it too.

Nor must the story of Jonah be taken literally. Regard the moral, and forget its fishy setting. Jesus Christ, indeed, referred to Jonah's sojourn in the "whale's belly" as typical of his own sojourn in the heart of the earth. But referring to a story is no proof of any belief in its truth. Not in the Bible. Jesus Christ also said, "Remember Lot's wife." But of course he did not believe the story literally. He used it for his own purpose. For the rest, he did not wish to unsettle men's minds by throwing doubt on such a time-honored narrative; besides, the time had not arrived to explain the chemical composition of rock-salt.

Witchcraft is a more serious matter. The Bible plainly says, "Thou shalt not suffer a witch to live." This text sealed the doom of millions of old women. It is the bloodiest text in all literature. The Jews believed in witchcraft, and the law against witches found its way into their sacred Scriptures. Sir Matthew Hale, a great English

22

judge and a good man, sentenced witches to be burnt in 1665, and said that he made no doubt at all that there were witches, for "the Scriptures had affirmed so much." Wesley, a century later, said that to give up witchcraft was to give up the Bible. Dr. Farrar sets down these facts honestly. He is also eloquent in reprobation of the cruelty inflicted on millions of "witches" in the Middle Ages. But he denies that the Bible is responsible for those infamies. "Witches" in the Bible may not mean witches, but "nefarious impostors." Good old wax nose again! Moreover, that ancient Jewish law was not binding upon Christians, and to make it so was "a gross misuse of the Bible." But how on earth could the Christians use it in any other way? The time came when men outgrew the superstition of witchcraft. Before that time they killed witches on Bible authority. Dr. Farrar himself, had he lived then, would have done the same. Living in a more enlightened age, he says that former Christians acted wrongly, and in fact diabolically. But what of the book which misled them? What of the book which, if it did not mislead them by design, harmonised so completely with their ignorant prejudices, and gave such a pious color to their unspeakable brutalities? Nor is this by any means the last word upon the subject. The witchcraft of the Old Testament has its counterpart in the demoniacal possession of the New Testament. Both are aspects of one and the same superstition.

The Bible *is* responsible for the cruel slaughter of millions of alleged witches. It is also responsible for the prolonged treatment of lunatics as possessed. The methods of science are now adopted in civilised countries. Hysterical women are no longer tortured as witches. Lunatics are no longer chained and beaten as persons inhabited by devils. Kindness and common sense have taken the place of cruelty and superstition. This change was brought about, not through the Bible, but in spite of it.

Sir Matthew Hale and John Wesley were at least honest. They were too sincere to deny the plain teaching of the Bible. Dr. Farrar represents a more enlightened, but a more hypocritical, form of Christianity. He sneers at "reconcilers" like Mr. Gladstone, who try to bolster up the Creation story as a scientific revelation. But is he not a "reconciler" himself in regard to miracles? And does he not play fast and loose with truth and honesty in his attempt to clear the Bible of its guilty responsibility in connection with that witch mania which is one of the darkest episodes in Christian history?

V. THE BIBLE AND FREETHOUGHT

The Bible may well be called the persecutor's text-book. It is difficult, if not impossible, to find in all its pages a single text in favor of real freedom of thought. Dr. Farrar champions what he calls "true Christianity," to which he declares that all persecution is entirely "alien." This "true Christianity" appears to depend upon "the spirit" of Christ, and seems to have little or no relation to the letter of Scripture. But what is the actual fact, when we view it in the light of history? In one of his lucid intervals of mere common sense, Dr. Farrar makes an important admission with regard to the worse than Armenian atrocities of the Jewish policy of extermination in Palestine. Those atrocities of cruelty and lust are said to have been ordered by God, but Dr. Farrar says that on this point the Jews were mistaken. They thought they were doing God a service, but they thought so ignorantly. And how was their ignorance corrected? Not by a special monition from heaven, but by the ordinary progress and elevation of the human mind. "It required," Dr. Farrar says, "but the softening influence of time and civilisation to obliterate in the best minds those fierce misconceptions." Precisely so. And is it anything but the softening influence of time and civilisation that makes Christians like Dr. Farrar ashamed of the bloody deeds of their co-religionists; which bloody deeds, by the way, have always been justified by appeals to the teachings of the Bible? Let there be no mistake on this point. Dr. Farrar himself does not scruple to write of the "deep damnation of deeds of deceit and sanguinary ferocity committed in the name of Holy Writ." "In some of their deadliest sins against the human race," he further says, "corrupted and cruel Churches have ever been most lavish in their appeals to Scripture." He admits that "the days are not far distant when it was regarded as a positive duty to put men

25

to death for their religious opinions," and that this was defended by Old Testament examples, and also by some texts from the New Testament. And it was "by virtue of texts like these" that enemies of the human race were "enabled" to combine the "garb and language of priests with the temper and trade of executioners."

Now, what has Dr. Farrar to urge *per contra?* Simply this: that the "early Christians" pleaded for toleration. "Force," they said, "is hateful to God." "It is no part of religion," said Tertullian, "to *compel* religion." But suppose all this be admitted—and there is much to be said by way of qualification—what does it amount to? The "early Christians" were in a minority. They did not yet command the sword of the magistrate. They could not persecute except by holding no fellowship with unbelievers, by shaking off the dust of their feet against those who rejected their Gospel, and by other harmless though detestable exhibitions of bigotry. They had to plead for their own existence, and in doing so they were obliged to appeal to the principle of general toleration. But the moment they triumphed, under Constantine, they began to flout the very principle to which they had formerly appealed. The humility of their weakness was more than equalled by the pride of their power. And what was the result? "From Augustine's days down to those of Luther," Dr. Farrar says, "scarcely one voice was raised in favor, I will not say of *tolerance*, but even of abstaining from fire and bloodshed in support of enforced uniformity." Dr. Farrar denounces in creditable language the frightful butcheries of Alva in the Netherlands, for which the Pope presented him with a jewelled sword bearing a pious inscription. He is properly horrified at the massacre of St. Bartholomew, in honor of which Pope Gregory XIII. struck a triumphant medal, and went in procession to sing a Te Deum to God, while the cannon thundered from the Castle of St. Angelo and bonfires blazed in the streets of Rome. He is bitter against the Church of Rome for its vast shedding of innocent blood. He reminds us that the infamous Holy Inquisition is still toasted by Catholic professors at Madrid; and that intolerance, having lost its power, has not lost its virulence, nor "ceased to justify its burning hatred by Scripture quotations." And he cites Manning's successor at Westminster, the truculent Cardinal Vaughan, as declaring with perfect approval that "the Catholic Church has never spared the knife, when necessary, to cut off rebels against her faith and authority."

But let it not be imagined that all the guilt of persecution rested upon the Church of Rome. Protestantism persecuted as freely as the Papacy. That heretics should be put down, and if necessary killed, was a principle common to both Churches. The question in dispute was, Which *were* the heretics? This is so incontestable that we need not fortify it with Protestant quotations and Protestant examples. It is not true, as Dr. Farrar alleges, that Luther "boldly proclaimed that thoughts are toll-free," if it is meant that he condemned persecution. Thoughts were toll-free against Romish exactions; that was what Luther meant. He held as strongly as any Papist that those who denied one essential doctrine of Christianity should be punished by the magistrates. He declared that reason always led to unbelief. He besought the Protestant princes to uphold "the faith" by every means in their power. And when the serfs rebelled, thinking that the "freedom" the Reformers talked about was to become a reality, it was Luther who wrote against them with unsurpassable ferocity, and advised that they should be "slaughtered like mad dogs."

Dr. Farrar rather judiciously refrains from mentioning Calvin in this connection, but in another part of the volume he refers to the great Genevian "reformer" in a somewhat gingerly manner. When the sins of Catholics have to be condemned he is quite dithyrambic; but when he has to censure the sins of Protestants he displays a most touching tenderness. Nothing could well be worse than the mixture of religious bigotry, personal spleen, and low duplicity, with which Calvin hunted Servetus to his fiery doom. Dr. Farrar sympathetically describes this vile act as an "error." He tries to satisfy his conscience, afterwards, by confessing that the Calvinists in general "were for the most part as severe to all who differed from them as they imagined God to be severe to the greater part of the human race."

Dr. Farrar's treatment of this subject is superficial. It is not a Bible text here or there which is the real basis of persecution. We advise him to read George Eliot's review of Lecky's *History of Rationalism*. He will then see that persecution is founded upon the fatal doctrine of salvation by faith. This doctrine makes the heretic more noxious than a serpent. A serpent poisons the body, a heretic poisons the soul. If it be true that his teaching may draw souls to hell, human welfare demands his extermination. Dr. Farrar does not disclaim this doctrine, and if he fails to act upon it he only betrays an amiable inconsistency. His heart is better than his head.

Dr. Farrar, like other Protestants, talks about the right of private judgment. But this is only fine and futile verbiage, unless he admits the sinlessness of intellectual error. If judgment depends on the will, it is through the will amenable to motives; consequently, the way to pro-mote correct opinions is to promise rewards and threaten punishments. But if judgment does not depend on the will; if it is necessarily determined by the laws of reason and evidence; then it is an absurdity to bribe and intimidate. Now there is no third alternative. One of these two theories must be right, and the other must be wrong. Dr. Farrar is logically bound to take his choice. If he believes that judgment depends on the will, he has no right to denounce persecution. If he believes that judgment does not depend on the will, he has no right to censure the most absolute freethought.

There are but two camps—the camp of Faith and the camp of Reason. Dr. Farrar belongs to the former. But he does not find his position comfortable. He casts a longing eye on the other camp. He wants to be in both. He therefore tries to form an alliance between them, if not to amalgamate them under one banner.

Reason, said Bishop Butler, is the only faculty wherewith we can judge of anything, even of revelation itself. Dr. Farrar quotes this statement with approval. He quotes similar sentences from other Protestant writers. Then he turns upon the Roman Church for keeping the Bible out of the hands of the people, and denounces it for this with ultra-Protestant vigor. He imagines that this is a vindication of Protestantism, at any rate relatively, as a champion of reason in opposition to blind faith and absolute authority. But *private* judgment and *free* judgment are not identical. When the Protestant puts an open Bible into your hands, and tells you to read it and judge of it for yourself, he is acting like a Freethinker; but when he proceeds to say that if you do not find it to be a divine book, and believe all its teaching about God, and Jesus Christ, and the Holy Ghost, and heaven and hell, you will infallibly be damned, he is acting like a Papist. His right of private judgment, at the finish, always means the right to differ from him on trivial points, and the duty of agreeing with him on every point which he chooses to regard as essential. If this is denied by Dr. Farrar, let him honestly answer this question—Is a Freethinker who has examined the Bible, and rejected it as a divine revelation, liable to any sort of penalty for his disbelief? The answer to this question will decide whether Dr. Farrar is really maintaining the rights of reason, or is merely maintaining the Protestant theory of faith against that of the Catholics, and standing up for the authority of the Book instead of the authority of the Church.

Meanwhile we venture to suggest that the Bible texts referred to by Dr. Farrar, as requiring us to exercise the right of private judgment, are very little to the point. "The spirit of man is the candle of the Lord" is a pretty text, but it does not seem to have much bearing on the issue. "Try the spirits" is all right in its way; but what if you find that *all* the spirits are illusions? "Prove all things" is good, but it must be taken with the context. Jesus indeed is reported to have said, "Why even of yourselves judge ye not what is right?" But he is also reported to have said, "He that believeth and is baptised shall be saved, and he that believeth not shall be damned."

By a judicious selection of texts you can prove anything from the Bible, and disprove anything—as Catholics have often reminded Protestants. To pick out passages that to some extent are favorable to a certain view, and to ignore much stronger passages that are

29

clearly opposed to it, may be an exercise of private judgment, and may satisfy the conscience of neo-Protestants of the school of Dr. Farrar; but it invites a contemptuous smile from Freethinkers who believe that Reason ought not to suffer such a prostitution.

We have to point out, finally, that Protestantism, with its open Bible, has everywhere maintained laws against blasphemy and heresy. The laws against heresy have fallen into desuetude in England, but while they lasted they were simply ferocious. We heard the late Lord Coleridge say from his seat in the Court of Queen's Bench, as Lord Chief Justice, that the Protestant laws against Roman Catholics, particularly in Ireland, where they were executed with remorseless ferocity, are without a parallel in the history of the world. Catholicism, however, is no longer under a ban. Even the Jews have been admitted to equal rights with their fellow citizens. But laws still remain in existence, and are occasionally put into operation, against "blasphemers." According to the language of common law indictments, it is a crime to bring the Holy Scripture or the Christian Religion into disbelief and contempt. It is true that many Christians are ready to profess a certain aversion to such laws, but they make no effort to repeal them. Many others contend that "blasphemy" is a question of manner, that the feelings of Christians should be protected, and that while men should not be punished for being Freethinkers, they should be punished for wounding orthodox susceptibilities. It is not proposed, however, that any limitations of taste or temper should be imposed upon Christian controversialists; and this contention may therefore be regarded as a subterfuge of bigotry. On the whole, it may be said that Catholics without the Bible, and Protestants with the Bible, persecute unbelief to the full extent of their opportunities; and it is only as toleration grows from other roots, and is nourished by other causes, that the Bibliolaters find out subtle interpretations of simple texts in favor of the prevailing tendency.

30

VI. MORALS AND MANNERS

Dr. Farrar takes the position that "the Bible is not homogeneous in its morality." There is a higher and a lower; and, to adopt the fine but paradoxical metaphor of Milton, within the lowest deep a lower deep still opens its dreadful abyss of crime and brutality. The same admission is made by Professor Bruce, [5] of the Free Church of Scotland; but this gentleman is more subtle than Dr. Farrar, and tries to save the reputation of the Bible by a notable piece of cauistical special-pleading. He does not allow, though he does not expressly deny, that the Bible contains any immorality. What he does is to draw a distinction between high morality and low morality. Immorality is sinning against your conscience. High morality is acting right up to its noblest dictates. Low morality is conduct in honest conformity to the low standard of a conscience but half-enlightened. When the prophetess Deborah sings triumphantly over the infamous exploit of Jael, who invited the fugitive Sisera into her tent, and assassinated him while he slept in the confidence of her hospitality, we must not say that either of these precious females was guilty of immorality. They were simply carrying out a low morality. And the same applies to Deborah's exclamation: "To every man a damsel or two"—meaning that the Jewish soldiers slew their male enemies and dragged home a brace of maidens each for themselves. Such conduct would be highly improper now, but it was all right then; at least it was as right as they knew; and we must not judge the actors by later ethical standards. So says Professor Bruce, and it would be true enough if the Bible were not put forward as a divine book, or if it ever reprehended the infamies of God's chosen people. But it does

---

[5] Christian Apologetics, p. 309.

31

nothing of the kind; it mentions Jael and Deborah in terms of absolute approval.

Dr. Farrar severely denounces the Jewish wars of extermination in Palestine, regardless of the fact—which is as true as any other religious fact in the Bible—that these atrocities were expressly commanded by Jehovah. Divines have defended the massacre of the Midianites, for instance, and the appropriation of their unmarried women; but Dr. Farrar calls their arguments "miserable pleas," and adds that if such "guilty and horrible" doings were "recorded without blame," it only shows that "the moral views of the desert tribes on such subjects were in this respect very rudimentary." These desert tribes were the chosen people of God; their prophets spoke under divine inspiration; yet even Jeremiah, in denouncing Moab, cries: "Cursed be he that keepeth back his sword from blood." According to Dr. Farrar, this proves how "slow" was the "development of the religious consciousness of mankind." But how did it happen that the Jews, with all the advantage of special inspiration, were just as slow in this respect as any other nation in the world's history? What is the use of "inspiration" if it does not appreciably quicken the natural development of the human conscience?

Many of the Bible heroes are fit for a distinguished place in the Newgate Calendar. Dr. Farrar himself cannot stomach "some details" in the lives of Abraham, Jacob, Jephthah, and David. Still, he urges that "the use made of them in the sceptical propaganda is often illegitimate." These worthies were not "faultless." It is their "general faithfulness" which is "rightly held up to admiration as our example." Faithfulness to what? Simply to their own greed and ambition, first of all, and secondly to the dominance of their tribal god Jehovah, who by such instruments triumphed over his rival dieties, and became at last the sole Lord God of Israel.

Dr. Farrar allows no palliating plea for the cursing Psalms. He cites a few of the very worst passages, black with hatred and red with blood, and asks: "Can the casuistry be anything but gross

32

which would palm off such passages as the very utterance of God?" Moses was "a great lawgiver and a great prophet," but Dr. Farrar will not "defend the divinity of passages so morally indefensible" as that, for instance, which gives the slave-owner impunity in killing his slave, provided he does not slay him on the spot, but beats him so that he dies "in a day or two." Nor is there "divinity" in the order to the Jews to refrain from eating bad meat, but to sell it to the Gentiles. Neither is there "divinity" in the order (Deut. xxi. 10-14) to take a wife for a month on trial. These things are parts of an ostensibly divine code, but lawgivers and people were alike mistaken. Inspiration did not guide them aright, but somehow or other it enables Dr. Farrar to correct their blunders three thousand years afterwards; which is merely saying, after all, that inspiration does not pioneer but follow the march of human progress.

During the reign of David a dreadful incident occurred. There had been a three years' famine, and David "inquired of the Lord." The answer was, "Blood upon Saul and upon his house!" Seven of Saul's sons were hung up "unto the Lord," and the famine was stopped. Dr. Farrar tells of an intelligent artisan who got up at a meeting and asked "whether it was not meant to imply that God was pacified by the blood of innocent human victims?" But he does not give the answer; and it either means this or it means nothing at all. In the same way, the story of Jephthah, who offered his daughter as a burnt-offering to the Lord, takes such an immolation for granted as a religious act of perfect propriety. Jephthah is mentioned as a hero of faith in the New Testament, and no hint is given that he acted wrongly in sacrificing his daughter on the altar of Jehovah.

We have said enough on this subject to give the reader a fair idea of Dr. Farrar's position. Let us now pass from Bible morals to Bible manners.

"The Bible," says Dr. Farrar, "is assailed on the ground that it contains coarse and unedifying stories." Take the story of Lot and his daughters, to say nothing of the bestial attempt on the angels in

Sodom. Could anything be more repulsive? Is there any excuse for putting such abominable feculence into the hands of children? After a lot of talk about it, and about, Dr. Farrar offers us the following most sapient observation: "The story of Lot wears a very different complexion if we regard it as an exhibition of unknown traditions about the connection between the Israelites and the tribes of Moab and Ammon." But what does this mean? The Moabites and Ammonites, according to the Bible, were hereditary enemies of the Jews, and it was impossible to exterminate them. They were evidently near of kin to the chosen people. Now, if these two facts are put together, it is easy to see the purpose of this story of Lot and his daughters. The Jews traced their own descent, in a perfectly honorable way, from Abraham and his legitimate wife Sarah, who are doubtless legendary characters. On the other hand, they traced the descent of the Moabites and Ammonites, their cousins and enemies, through the no less legendary Lot and his two daughters, thus throwing the aspersion of incest upon the cradle of both those races. This is the adequate and satisfactory explanation of the story. It is an exhibition of dirty and unscrupulous hatred; and, as such, it is a curious fragment of "the Word of God."

Take next what Dr. Farrar calls "the pathetic story of Hosea," the prophet who was ordered by God to marry a prostitute—not to use the more downright language of the English Bible. Dr. Farrar suggests that there is some doubt as to the meaning of the original. Hosea's wife may have turned out a baggage after the nuptials, instead of being one before. "It was the anguish caused by her infidelity," he says, "that first woke Hosea to the sense of Israel's infidelity to Jehovah." And read in the light of this "modern criticism" the story of Hosea is "in the highest degree pure and noble." How pretty! All that remains for Dr. Farrar to do is to explain away as equally "pure and noble" the imagery of Ezekiel in reference to Aholah and Aholibah. There is no reason why "modern criticism" in the hands of gentlemen like Dr. Farrar should not transform Priapus into a Sunday-school teacher.

Not only are there very gross stories in the Bible, many of which are too beastly to dwell upon, but its language is often gratuitously disgusting. And every scholar knows that the Hebrew text is sometimes far more "purple" than our English version. Dr. Farrar admits that if the "exact meaning" of certain passages were understood, they "could not be read without a blush." "Happily," he says, they are "disguised by the euphemisms of translations." That is to say, the inspired Bible writers, or penmen of the Holy Ghost, as old divines called them, were often indecent and sometimes positively obscene. Dr. Farrar's explanation is, that "ancient and Eastern readers" were not easily shocked, and that our modern "sensibility" is of "recent growth." But this proves again that "inspiration" is in no sense the cause of progress, and does not anticipate it in the slightest degree.

"The Bible," Dr. Farrar says, "is inextricably mingled with all that is greatest in human history." This is a fair specimen of his roystering style. We presume he has contracted it through long years of preaching from the coward's castle of the pulpit, where a man can exaggerate as much as he pleases without the slightest fear of contradiction. Dr. Farrar does not say that the Bible is mixed up with *much* of the greatest in human history; no, it must be mixed up with *all* the greatest—which is a transparent falsehood and a no less transparent absurdity. What did Greece and Rome owe to the Bible? Absolutely nothing. There is no evidence that they were acquainted with any part of the Old Testament, and Greece had become a mere name before a line of the New Testament was written. Some of the greatest things in the world were done and said by the "heathen." Greek philosophy, Greek literature, Greek art, are imperishable. Roman jurisprudence and Roman government are the basis of every civilised polity. Plutarch's heroes are all Pagans, and let Dr. Farrar match them if he can in the history of Christendom.

Dr. Farrar calls the Bible "the statesman's manual," but he judiciously refrains from showing that statesmen ever act upon its teaching; indeed, he spends a great deal of time in showing that they ought *not* to act upon its teaching, unless they carefully avoid the obvious "letter," and allow themselves to be influenced by the recondite "spirit." For instance, it is perfectly clear that the Bible does not contain a single word against slavery; it is also perfectly clear to all who possess a tincture of scholarship that many of its references to slavery are fraudulently translated. "Servants obey your masters" really means "Slaves obey your owners." Moreover, the Bible contains precise regulations of slavery. God did not tell the Jews that holding slaves was infamous, that man could never have honest property in human flesh and blood. He allowed them to buy and sell Gentiles at their pleasure. He permitted them to enslave their own countrymen for a period of seven years, and in certain cases "for ever." Even in the New Testament we find St Paul sending back a runaway slave to his master. True, he sent with the slave a touching letter to the slave-owner, but sending him back at all was giving a sanction to the institution. Dr. Farrar admits that American pulpits "rang with incessant Scriptural defences of slavery." He quotes from a Southern bishop, who described slavery as "a curse and a blight," yet declared it to be "recognised by the Bible," so that "every man has a right to his own slaves, provided they are not treated with unnecessary cruelty." Dr. Farrar asks whether there was ever "a stranger utterance on the lips of a Christian bishop." He calls this "distorting the Bible." But he does not prove the distortion. He calmly assumes it. He cannot deny the existence of all those slavery texts in the Bible. All he can do is to say that what was "relatively excusable" among the Jews is at present "execrable," and is now "absolutely and for ever wrong." Very good; but how was that discovered? Not by reading the Bible. The Jews read the Bible, the early Christians read the Bible, just as well as Dr. Farrar, but they did not find that it condemned slavery. Dr. Farrar lives in a later age, in the light of a higher civilisation. He therefore *reads into* the Bible whatever it *ought to* contain as the word of God. He does not scruple to override explicit texts by more or less arbitrary deductions from vague maxims and ejaculations. He pretends that the "spirit" of the Bible in some way wrought the abolition of slavery. But every well-informed student is aware that the abolition of slavery depended upon economical conditions. We *outgrow* slavery by advancing beyond it in the process of industrial development, and when we *have* outgrown it we regard it with abhorrence. When the institution is in the way of being supplanted by a higher form of productive labor, the moral revolt against it begins, growing in strength and intensity as the economical change approaches its climax. It was natural that the anti-slavery movement in America should take place in the

37

Northern States, where the conditions favourable to slavery did not exist as they did in the Southern States. We may be pardoned for supposing that if Dr. Farrar's lot had been cast in a Southern State he would have defended slavery as a Bible institution. He is preaching now after its abolition, when denunciation of it is cheap and easy, and is no particular credit to the preacher's religion. While slavery existed in America, it was at first justified by the Bible in all parts of the Union. Northern abolitionists at last found that the Bible did not teach slavery after all; but this did not alter the view of the Southern slaveholders and the Southern Churches. Here again we see the force of the Catholic taunt that Protestants can prove anything, and disprove anything, by appealing to texts in such a composite book as the Bible. Here again we also see that the Bible never *instigates* any step in the march of human improvement.

Dr. Farrar waxes eloquent, after his special fashion, over the glories of England in the age of Elizabeth. He attributes them all to the "open Bible," which was then placed in the hands of the people. Of course they had nothing to do with the new astronomy, the discovery of America, and the invention of printing! Such paltry causes as these cannot enter into competition with the might and majesty of the Bible! Still, we may venture to remind Dr. Farrar that these Englishmen of the Elizabethan age, with the "open Bible" in their hands, went and started the African slave trade. Evidently they did not read in it then, as Dr. Farrar does now, any condemnation of that horrible business. They worked it for all it was worth. England, with the "open Bible" in its hand, continued to do so for another two hundred years. One of the chief centres of the slave trade was the pious city of Bristol. It grew rich on the abominable traffic. Slavery has been abolished, but the old odor of piety still clings to the city of Bristol. Its merchants fattened on the slave trade with the "open Bible" in their hands. They now subscribe to missionary societies to convert the blacks, and they still stick to the "open Bible." It was good for upholding black slavery, and it is still good for upholding white slavery.

All that we have said about slavery applies in its degree to

38

polygamy. Both institutions are sanctioned by the Bible, and the pleas of the "Higher Criticism" in relation to the one are just as hollow as they are in relation to the other. We may go farther and say that the Bible is very far from being woman's best friend, as it is often represented. It starts by making her the Devil's first customer, and the introducer of sin and death; it continues to hold her as inferior and subject to man, lumping her in the tenth commandment with the house, the ox, and the ass, as the man's property; and, finally, in the New Testament, it expressly tells her that her duty is to be silent and submissive, for the husband is the head of the wife as Christ is the head of the Church.

We need not follow Dr. Farrar in his rhapsodical references to the various achievements of the Bible. We may remark, however, that his reference to Japan is singularly unhappy. That country *has* accepted the leading ideas of Western civilisation, but it has *not* accepted Christianity. Nor is Dr. Farrar well advised in laying so much stress on the Pilgrim Fathers. He says that they had a preference for the "pure, unadulterated lessons of the Bible." Perhaps they had. But what were those lessons as illustrated by their actions? Certainly intolerance was one of them. They had no conception of religious liberty. "The Pilgrim Fathers," as Sir Walter Besant remarks in his little book on *The Rise of the Empire*, "believed that everybody should think as they themselves thought. Had they achieved their own way, they would have sent Laud himself, and all who thought like him, across the ocean with the greatest alacrity." They also believed in witchcraft, probably because Dr. Farrar was not at hand to explain that the Bible did not mean what it said; and they tortured and burnt witches with remarkable gusto.

It would also be a waste of time to correct all Dr. Farrar's statements about the influence of the Bible in other directions. We will take a single illustration of his fantastical method. He tells us that the Bible "inspired the pictures of Fra Angelico and Raphael, the music of Handel and Mendelssohn." Perhaps he will tell us whether it inspired Raphael's picture of the Fornarina, and why it

39

did not inspire the music of Beethoven and Wagner. Both those great composers, as a matter of fact, were "infidels."

Nothing could be more absurd than orthodox talk about the Bible "inspiring" great poets, artists, and musicians. Men of genius are inspired by nature. Their inspiration is born with them. It cannot be made; it can only be utilised. All that religions have done is to employ the genius they could not create. Every religion has done this in turn. The genius was there always as a natural endowment. It existed before all the world's religions, and it will outlive them.

VIII. INSPIRATION

The Higher Criticism, as expounded by Dr. Farrar, admits nearly all the Bible difficulties that have been advanced by "infidels." Let us recapitulate the most important. The Bible is hopelessly at variance with science. It sometimes contradicts well-established history. Many of its stories, taken literally, are obviously absurd. Some of the actions it records with apparent approval are wicked or disgusting. A good deal of its language sins against common decency. Several books were not written by the authors whose names they bear. Others are, and must for ever remain, anonymous. The dates of composition of the various books are not what has been generally supposed. Occasionally the true chronology differs from the received chronology by many centuries. To the great majority of readers the Bible has never been known, and never can be known, except in translations. No translation can possibly be perfect. Every translation of the Bible is known to contain grave and numerous errors. Even in the original Hebrew and Greek manuscripts there are thousands of various readings. In some cases the text is uncertain, in some cases interpolated, and in others irrecoverably impaired. The vowel points by which Hebrew is now read are demonstrably a modern invention. Even the discourses of Jesus Christ, in the New Testament, are not reported with accuracy. The New Testament writers seldom quote from the Old Testament exactly, but generally rely upon the Greek translation called the Septuagint.

Sometimes they quote passages which are not in Scripture at all. "Out of 288 passages quoted from the Old Testament in the New," says Dr. Farrar, "there are but 53 which agree accurately with the original Hebrew. In 76 the New Testament differs both from the

Greek and the Hebrew; and in 99 the New Testament, the Greek, and the Hebrew are all variant."

On the face of it, then, the Bible is doomed. A book of which all these things can be said, without the slightest fear of contradiction, must sooner or later be dropped as the Word of God. It will be recognised as a human composition.

Meanwhile, those who live by the Bible, and are professionally interested in its "supremacy," as Dr. Farrar calls it, cast about a for means of giving it a fresh reputation. The old conception of it is fatally discredited; a new one may give it a fresh lease of life.

Evidently there is only one direction open to the theological trimmers. They must start another theory of inspiration—one that will conserve the "sacred" character of the Bible in spite of every difficulty that has been, or can be discovered.

The Bible is no longer to be called *the* Word of God. Ruskin says, and Dr. Farrar seems to quote it approvingly, that "it is a grave heresy (or wilful source of division) to call any book, or collection of books, the Word of God." Ten pages later, however, we are told that the Bible, as a whole, *may* be spoken of as the Word of God, because it "contains words and messages of God to the human soul." This word "contains" is the magical spell by which Dr. Farrar seeks to dissipate all difficulties. He finds the expression in the Church Articles, in the Book of Homilies, and in the Shorter Catechism. But in order to see how illegitimate is Dr. Farrar's use of these authorities, let us take his extract from the last of them: "The Word of God which is *contained* in the Scriptures of the Old and New Testament is the only rule to direct us how we may enjoy and glorify Him." Is it not clear that the word "*contained*" is used here in its primary meaning? Did not the writers mean that the Word of God is included or comprehended in the Old and New Testament only, and is not to be found elsewhere? Would they not have been shocked to hear a clergyman of the Church of England say that some parts of the Bible were *not* the Word of God? If so, their use of the word "contain" lends no countenance to the use made of it by

42

Dr. Farrar. And is it not a shallow trick upon our intelligence to argue that different persons, using the same word, necessarily mean the same thing? Words are the money of fools, as Hobbes said, but only the counters of wise men. We must get at the actual value of the thing which is symbolised. And the moment we do this, we see that Dr. Farrar's theory of the Word of God is *not* the same as that of the gentlemen who drew up the Shorter Catechism. They would indeed have laughed at his "contains," and excommunicated and imprisoned him, and perhaps burnt him at the stake. It is not by torturing one poor word ten thousand ways that such wide differences can be reconciled.

Passing by this ridiculous legerdemain, let us take Dr. Farrar's theory for what it is worth. The Bible *contains* the Word of God. But how are we to find it? What is the criterion by which we are to separate God's word from man's word? Dr. Farrar bids us use "the ordinary means of criticism and spiritual discernment." But such a vague generality is nothing but verbiage. What we want is the *criterion*. Now the nearest approach to it in all Dr. Farrar's pages is the following:—

"Is it not a plain and simple rule that anything in the Bible which teaches, or is misinterpreted to teach, anything which is not in accordance with the love, the gentleness, the truthfulness of Christ's Gospel, is *not* God's word to us, however clearly it stands on the page of Scripture?"

This is at best a *negative* criterion; and, on close examination, it turns out to be no criterion at all. The criterion, to be valid, must be *external* to the book itself. Dr. Farrar's criterion is *internal*. He picks out one part of the Bible as the standard for judging all the rest. This is entirely arbitrary. Moreover, it would soon be found impossible in practice. Dr. Farrar's criterion may be "plain," but it is not so "simple," except in the uncomplimentary sense of the word. For "Christ's Gospel," by which the rest of the Bible is to be tried, is itself a very composite and self-contradictory thing. Further, if all that agrees with Christ's Gospel is the Word of God, is it not superfluous as being a mere repetition? Dr. Farrar would therefore bring the actual, valid Word of God within the compass of the Four Gospels; dismissing all the rest, like the Arabian Caliph who commanded a whole library to be burnt on the ground that if the books differed from the Koran they were pernicious, and if they agreed with it they were useless. Nor is this all. Dr. Farrar admits that the discourses of Jesus Christ are not reported with accuracy. Therefore, having made the Gospels the criterion of the Word of God in the rest of the Bible, he would be obliged to select some special passages as the criterion of the Word of God in the rest of the Gospels. This is what Shakespeare would call a world-without-end process.

Candidly, it seems to us that if the Bible *is* not the Word of God, but only *contains* the Word of God—that is to say, if it is partly God's word and partly man's word—the clergy of all denominations should unite in publishing a Bible with the divine and human parts clearly specified by being printed in different types. And surely, if the Bible is in any sense inspired, it should be possible, by a new and final act of inspiration, to settle this distinction for ever.

Allowing the clergy to meditate this holy enterprise, we proceed to consider Dr. Farrar's theory of inspiration. Of course he discards the old theory of verbal dictation; indeed, he calls it "irreverent," because it attributes to God what modern men of intelligence and good manners would be ashamed to own. He even quarrels with the very term inspiration as "vague," and says it would be "a boon if some less ambiguous word could be adopted." Four theories, he says, have been entertained in the Christian Church. The first is the *mechanical* theory, which implies that the Holy Ghost dictated, and the inspired penmen were merely his amanuenses. The second is the *dynamic*, which recognises "the indefeasible guidance of the Holy Spirit." The third is that of *illumination*, which confines the divine guidance to matters of faith and doctrine. The fourth is that of *general* inspiration, which regards the Holy Spirit as influencing the writers in the same way as it influences "other noble and holy

44

souls." This fourth theory is the one which Dr. Farrar himself affects. Every pure and sweet influence upon the human soul, he says, is a heavenly inspiration. We owe to it "all that is best and greatest in philosophy, eloquence, and song." Haydn said of his grandest chorus in the "Creation": "Not from me but from above it all has come!" "There is inspiration," says Dr. Farrar, "whenever the spirit of God makes itself heard in the heart of man." Apparently — for we can never be quite sure of Dr. Farrar — the only superiority of the Bible lies in the fact that "the voice of God" speaks to us "far more intensely" out of it than out of "any [other?] form of human speech."

Such a theory of inspiration is too vague and universal. Sooner than give up inspiration altogether Dr. Farrar is prepared to share it all round. But is not proving too much as bad as proving too little? If the Bible is only inspired — where it *is* inspired — in the same sense as other books are inspired; if the difference is not one of kind, but simply of degree; then it is really idle to talk about its inspiration any longer. The word *inspiration* loses all its original meaning. It becomes a poetical expression, implying nothing supernatural, but merely the exaltation of natural powers and faculties. God is then behind the Bible only as God is behind everything; and Christianity, ceasing to be a special revelation, becomes only a certain form of Theism.

This loose theory of *general* inspiration will doubtless serve the present turn of the clergy, who have to face a general and growing dissatisfaction with the Bible. But it cannot live very long in a scientific age. It will be found out in time, like all the Bible theories that preceded it. The first Protestant dogma was the infallibility of Scripture. That was exploded by modern science and textual criticism. Then came the dogma of plenary inspiration, which had a comparatively short-lived existence, as it was only the old dogma of infallibility in disguise. Next came the dogma of illumination, which may be said to have begun with Coleridge and ended with Maurice. Finally, we have the dogma of general inspiration, which began nowhere and ends nowhere, which means anything or

45

nothing, and which is a sort of "heads we win, tails you lose" theory in the hands of the clever expounders of the Higher Criticism.

Behind the last, as well as the first, of all these theories of inspiration stands the fatal objection of Thomas Paine, that inspiration, to be real, must be personal. A man may be sure that God speaks to him, but how can he be sure that God has spoken to another man? He may think it possible or probable, but he can never be certain. What is revelation at first-hand, said Paine, is only hearsay at second-hand. Real inspiration, therefore, eventuates in mysticism. The inner light shines, the inner voice speaks; God holds personal communication with the individual soul. Each believer carries what the author of *Hudibras* calls "the dark lanthorn of the spirit," which "none see by but those who bear it." And the very multiplicity and diversity of the oracle's deliverances are a proof that in all of them man is speaking to himself. He questions his gods, and hears only the echo of his own voice.

IX. THE TESTIMONY OF JESUS

Some of the teaching of the Higher Criticism as to the authorship and credibility of the Old Testament is, on the face of it, contrary to the plain language of Jesus Christ himself in the Gospels. Moses, for instance, is no longer considered as the author of the Pentateuch. Canon Driver, who is perhaps the chief scholar of this movement in the Church of England, as Dean Farrar is perhaps its chief rhetorician, locates the composition of the book of Deuteronomy in the period between Isaiah and Jeremiah. Throughout the book, he observes, the writer introduces Moses in the third person, and puts speeches in his mouth which of course he never uttered. But in "framing discourses appropriate to Moses' situation!" he was not guilty of "forgery," for he was "doing nothing inconsistent with the literary usages of his age and people." That is to say, everybody did it, and this writer was no worse than his contemporaries—which is probably true. But passing by the question of casuistry here involved, we repeat that the Mosaic authorship of the Pentateuch is entirely abandoned. Dr. Farrar is quite as emphatic as Dr. Driver on this point. He denies that there is "any proof of the existence of a *collected* Pentateuch earlier than the days of Ezra (b.c. 444)"—a thousand years after the time of Moses. He points out that the salient features of the so-called Mosaic Law, such as the Passover, the Sabbatical year, and the Day of Atonement, are not to be traced in the old historical books or in the earlier prophets. Nor does he scruple to assert that the Pentateuch is "a work of composite structure," which has been "edited and re-edited several times," and "contains successive strata of legislation." In the New Testament, however, Moses is repeatedly spoken of as the author of the Pentateuch. [6] Not to multiply texts, for in such a case one is as good

---

[6] Matthew xix. 7, 8; Mark x. 3, 4; xii. 26; Luke xvi. 29-31; Luke xx. 37; John v. 45, 46; vii. 19, 22, 23.

as a thousand, we will take a decisive passage in the fourth Gospel:—

"Do not think that I will accuse you to the Father. There is one that accuseth you, even Moses, in whom ye trust. For had ye believed Moses, ye would have believed me: for he wrote of me. But if ye believe not his writings, how shall ye believe my words?" (John v. 45-47).

The speaker in this instance is Christ himself. It is he, and not the evangelist, who speaks of the writings of Moses, and declares that Moses "wrote of me."

Now let us turn to the book of Psalms, which has been well called the Hymn Book of the Second Temple. According to Dr. Farrar, they are "a collection of sacred poems in five separate books of very various antiquity." Canon Driver points out that they are mostly posterior to the prophetical writings. "When the Psalms," he says, "are compared with the prophets, the latter seem to show, on the whole, the greater originality; the psalmists, in other words, *follow* the prophets, appropriating and applying the truths which the prophets proclaimed." Very few of the Psalms are earlier than the seventh century before Christ. Dr. Driver affirms this with "tolerable confidence." Dr. Farrar says that "some may mount to an epoch earlier than David's," but this is mere conjecture. The more cautious Dr. Driver will not commit himself further than "a verdict of *non liquet*"; that is to say, there is no proof that David did not write one or two of the Psalms, and no evidence that he did. His name was associated with the collection, in the same way as the name of Solomon was associated with the Proverbs. Nevertheless it is David who is referred to by Jesus as the author of the hundred-and-tenth Psalm. [7] But this Psalm is one of those which are allowed to belong to a much later period. Jesus quoted it as David's, but Professor Sanday says "it seems difficult to believe it really came

---

[7] Matthew xxii. 43-45; Mark xii. 36, 37; Luke xx. 42-44.

from him" [8]—which is as strong an expression as a Christian divine could be expected to permit himself in a case of such delicacy.

We have already seen that the book of Daniel was not written by the prophet Daniel, but by some unknown author hundreds of years later, probably in the second century before Christ. Upon this subject Professor Sanday takes precisely the same view as Canon Driver. He says that this is "the critical view" and has "won the day." All the facts support the "supposition that the book was written in the second century b.c.," and not "in the sixth." "The real author," he says, "is unknown," and "the name of Daniel is only assumed." He was writing, not a history, but a homily, to encourage his brethren at the time of the Maccabean struggle. "To this purpose of his," Professor Sanday says, "there were features in the traditional story of Daniel which appeared to lend themselves; and so he took that story and worked it up in the way which seemed to him most effective." Jesus Christ, however, held the orthodox view of his own time, and spoke of Daniel as the actual author of this book (Matthew xxiv. 15). "But this," Professor Sanday observes, "it is right to say, is only in one Gospel, where the mention of Daniel may be an insertion of the Evangelist's." Such conjectural shifts are Christian critics reduced to in their effort to minimise difficulties; as though *reducing* the mistakes of Jesus in any way saved his *infallibility*.

We will now turn to some portions of the Old Testament narrative which the Higher Criticism regards as legendary, but which Jesus regarded as strictly historical. One of these is the story of the Flood. No one of any standing is now prepared to defend this story, at least as we find it in the book of Genesis. A few orthodox scientists, like Sir James W. Dawson, pour out copious talk about tremendous floods in former geological ages; but what has this to do with the Bible narrative of a universal deluge which occurred

---

[8] Professor W. Sanday, Bampton Lectures on Inspiration, p. 409. Canon Gore, with this utterance of Jesus right before him, still more emphatically denies that this Psalm was, or could have been, composed by David. See his Bampton Lectures on The Incarnation of the Son of God, p. 197.

49

some four thousand five hundred years ago? The Higher Critics have the impatience of Freethinkers with such intellectual charlatanry. They regard the story of the Flood as a Jewish legend, which was not even original, but borrowed from the superstitions of Babylon. Yet the opinion of Jesus Christ seems to have been very different. Here are his own words:—

"But as the days of Noe were, so shall also the coming of the Son of Man be. For as in the days that were before the flood they were eating and drinking, marrying and giving in marriage, until the day that Noe entered into the ark, and knew not until the flood came, and took them all away, so shall also the coming of the Son of man be" (Matthew xxiv. 37-39).

Jesus Christ appears to have believed, like the disciples he was addressing, like all the rest of his countrymen, and like nearly all Christians until very recently, that the Flood was an historical occurrence, that Noah and his family were saved in the ark, and that all the other inhabitants of the world were drowned.

Another story which the Higher Criticism dismisses as legendary is that of Jonah. The book in which it is related was, of course, not written by Jonah, the son of Amittai, of whom we read in 2 Kings xiv. 25, and who lived in the reign of Jeroboam II. "It cannot," as Dr. Driver says, "have been written until long after the lifetime of Jonah himself." Its probable date is the fifth century before Christ. Dr. Driver says it is "not strictly historical "—that is to say, the events recorded in it never happened. Jonah was not really entertained for three days in a whale's belly, nor did his preaching convert the whole city of Nineveh. The writer's purpose was didactic; he wished to rebuke the exclusiveness of his own people, and to teach them that God's care extended, at least occasionally, to other nations as well as the Jews. Some critics, such as Cheyne and Wright, regard the story as allegorical; Jonah standing for Israel, the whale for Babylon, and the vomiting up of the prophet for the return of the Jews from exile. Dr. Farrar draws attention to the "remarkable" fact that in the book of Kings "no allusion is made to any mission or adventure of the historic Jonah." He adds that there is not "the faintest trace of his mission or its results amid the masses of Assyrian inscriptions." Even the writer of the book of Jonah, according to Dr. Farrar, attached "no importance" to its "supernatural incidents," which "only belong to the allegorical form of the story." So much for the Higher Critics; and now let us hear Jesus Christ:—

"An evil and adulterous generation seeketh after a sign; and there shall no sign be given to it, but the sign of the prophet Jonas: For as Jonas was three days and three nights in the whale's belly; so shall the Son of man be three days and three nights in the heart of the earth. The men of Nineveh shall rise in judgment with this generation, and shall condemn it: because they repented at the preaching of Jonas; and behold a greater than Jonas is here" (Matthew xii. 39-41).

This utterance of Jesus is also reported in Luke (xi. 29-32), but with an important variation, the reference to Jonah in the whale's belly being entirely omitted. This variation is seized upon by Dr. Farrar. The fishy reference, he says, occurs in Matthew *alone*, and it may "represent a comment or marginal note by the Evangelist, or of some other Christian teacher." This, however, is an arbitrary supposition, which everyone is free to repudiate; and Dr. Farrar feels obliged to add that "even if our Lord did allude to the whale" it does not follow that we should regard it as "literal history." But this is not the question at issue. The real question is, did Jesus Christ believe the story of Jonah and the whale? If he did not, it must be admitted that he had a most unfortunate way of expressing himself.

No educated Christian in the present age believes the story of Lot's wife being changed into a pillar of rock salt, although Josephus pretended that he had seen it, and many travellers and pilgrims have searched for it as a sacred relic. Jesus Christ, however, gave great prominence to this salted lady. "Remember Lot's wife" is a verse by itself in the Protestant Bible (Luke xvii. 32).

51

Jesus also refers to the rain of fire and brimstone by which Sodom was destroyed.

Here then, upon the face of it, we have Jesus Christ's testimony to three documents as having been written by men who did not write them, and to the historical character of three incidents which are purely fabulous. Now the Higher Criticism must be wrong, or else Jesus Christ was mistaken; in other words, he was not infallible, and therefore not God. But the Higher Critics declare that they are not wrong; they also declare that Jesus Christ was not mistaken. Let us see how they try to save their own accuracy and his infallibility.

We must remark, in passing, that some of these critics hint, without exactly asserting, that Jesus *may* have been mistaken. Dr. Farrar bids us remember that "by the very fact of taking our nature upon him Christ voluntarily submitted himself to human limitations." There were some things which, as a man, he did not know. Yes, but he was also God; and the conjunction of "knowledge" and "ignorance" in one person, and with respect to a single subject, would dissolve the unity of the God-man, which is a dogma of Christian theology. Moreover, as Canon Liddon argued, it is not so much a question of Christ's omniscience as a question of his infallibility. Supposing there were some matters, such as the date of the day of judgment, of which he was ignorant; he might confess his ignorance or remain silent, and no harm would accrue to anyone; but if he spoke upon any matter, and was mistaken through want of knowledge, he would become a propagator of error; and this would not only destroy the doctrine of his deity, but very seriously impair his authority as a teacher, and cause everything he said to be open to the gravest suspicion. No less dangerous is it to fall back upon the explanation that "the discourses of Christ are not reproduced by the Evangelists with verbal identity"—to use Dr. Farrar's own language. Dr. Sanday seems a little attracted by this explanation. He reminds us that, whatever views Jesus himself entertained as to the Scriptures of the Old Testament, his views have come down to us through the medium of persons who shared the erroneous ideas that were then current on the subject. We must be prepared, he says, for the possibility that Christ's sayings in regard to it "have not been reported with absolute accuracy." But after all "not much allowance" should be made for this; which means, we suspect, that the worthy Professor saw the dreadful peril of pursuing this vein of observation, and desisted from it before he had said enough to cause serious mischief.

The more astute Higher Critics avoid such dangers. They resort to a theory that combines mystery and plausibility, by which they hope to satisfy believers on both sides of their natures. Dr. Farrar tells us that Christ, to become a man, emptied himself of his glory; and that this "examination" involved the necessity of speaking as a man to men. This position is perhaps best expressed by Canon Gore:—

"It is contrary to his whole method to reveal his Godhead by any anticipations of natural knowledge. The Incarnation was a self-emptying of God to reveal himself under conditions of human nature, and from the human point of view. We are able to draw a distinction between what he revealed and what he used......Now when he speaks of the 'sun rising' he is using ordinary human knowledge. Thus he does not reveal his eternity by statements as to what had happened in the past, or was to happen in the future, outside the ken of existing history. He made his Godhead gradually manifest by his attitude towards men and things about him, by his moral and spiritual claims, by his expressed relation to his father, not by any miraculous exemptions of himself from the conditions of natural knowledge in its own proper province. Thus the utterances of Christ about the Old Testament do not seem to be nearly definite or clear enough to allow of our supposing that in this case he is departing from the general method of the Incarnation, by bringing to bear the unveiled omniscience of the Godhead, to anticipate or foreclose a development of natural knowledge." [9]

This would perhaps be sublime if it were only intelligible. We are

---

[9] Rev. Charles Gore, Lux Mundi (seventh edition), pp. 360, 361.

not surprised at Dr. Driver's turning away from the metaphysics of this theory. His mind is cast in a more sober and practical mould. It is enough for him that the aim of Christ's teaching was a religious one; that he naturally accepted, as the basis of his teaching, the opinions respecting the Old Testament that were current around him; that he did not raise "issues for which the time was not yet ripe, and which, had they been raised, would have interfered seriously with the paramount purpose of his life."[10]

This is excellently said. It is just what Paley might have written in present-day circumstances. But it contains no note of the supernatural. It deals with Jesus as a mere man, who did not disclose all the information he possessed, but sometimes veiled his knowledge for temporary reasons. It leaves his Godhead in the background. It does not recognise how easy it was for Omnipotence to act differently. And when the Higher Criticism points out that the human mind could, in the course of time, free itself from errors as to the authorship and credibility of the Old Testament, it forgets that Jesus Christ, by accommodating himself to those errors, *perpetuated* them. His authority was appealed to for centuries—it is appealed to now—in favor of falsehood. Nor is this falsehood trivial and innocuous. It has been extremely harmful. It has fostered a wrong view of the Bible, it has prolonged the reign of superstition, and thus hindered the growth of true civilisation. This is an impeachment of the moral character of Jesus. It is a confession that he served a temporary object at the expense of the permanent interests of humanity. We feel constrained, therefore, to admit the force of the words of Canon Liddon:—

"We have lived to hear men proclaim the legendary and immoral character of considerable portions of those Old Testament scriptures, upon which our Lord has set the seal of his infallible authority. And yet, side by side with this rejection of Scriptures so deliberately sanctioned by Christ, there is an unwillingness which, illogical as it is, we must sincerely welcome, to profess any explicit

---

[10] Introduction, Preface, xix.

rejection of the Church's belief in Christ's divinity. Hence arises the endeavour to intercept a conclusion, which might otherwise have seemed so plain as to make arguments in its favor an intellectual impertinence. Hence a series of singular refinements, by which Christ is presented to the modern world as really Divine, yet as subject to fatal error; as Founder of the true religion, yet as the credulous patron of a volume replete with worthless legends; as the highest Teacher and Leader of humanity, yet withal as the ignorant victim of the prejudices and follies of an unenlightened age." [11]

Canon Gore devotes several pages of his Bampton Lectures to this subject, but he does not fairly answer the straightforward objections raised by Canon Liddon. Dealing with the references of Jesus to the Mosaic authorship of the Pentateuch, and to Jonah's three days' entombment in the whale's belly, and with the argument that this endorsement by Jesus "binds us to receive these narratives as simple history," he blandly declares, "To this argument I do not think that we need yield." Of course not. There is no need to yield to anything you do not like; for this is a free country, at least to Christians. But what is the logical conclusion? That is the point to be decided. Canon Gore does not face it; he merely expresses a personal disinclination. Subsequently he pleads that "a heavy burden" should not be laid on "sensitive consciences," and that men should not be asked "to accept as matter of revelation what seems to them an improbable literary theory." But this again is a personal appeal. These men must be left to attend to their own consciences. They have no right to demand a suppression of truth, or a perversion of logic, for their particular advantage.

When a candid reader has finished all that the Higher Criticism has to say on this matter, we believe he will be filled with a sense of its insincerity. It never strikes a note of triumph, or even a note of conviction. It is timid, furtive, and apologetic; and shelters itself against reason by plunging into mystery. In place of all the difficulties it removes it sets up a colossal one of its own

---

[11] Canon H. P. Liddon, The Divinity of Christ (fourteenth edition), p. 462.

manufacture; the difficulty, to wit, of conceiving that God himself lent a sanction to grave and far-reaching error as to his own Word; or what would inevitably be regarded as a sanction, and would necessarily delay for many hundreds of years the discovery and reception of the truth. The Higher Criticism, in short, has supplied a new argument against the deity of Jesus Christ.

X. THE BIBLE AND
THE CHURCH OF ENGLAND

Dr. Farrar's book has naturally given offence to the more orthodox Christians. Clergymen like "Father" Ignatius stigmatise him, and indeed all clerical exponents of the Higher Criticism, as wolves in sheeps' clothing, who eat the Church's meat and do the work of "infidelity." We are not surprised, therefore, that some reassurance has been deemed necessary; nor astonished that it took the form of a popular announcement in the newspapers. Some months ago—to be accurate, it was in September—the following paragraph went the round of the press:—

"Dean Farrar and the Scriptures.—A correspondent called the attention of Dean Farrar to the fact that Atheistic lecturers are in the habit of affirming that he does not believe in the Bible (referring to his works as a confirmation of the statement), and observed that, if such a grave assertion were allowed to be propagated without contradiction, the young and the ignorant might be deceived by it. The Dean, who is at present staying in Yorkshire, replied as follows: 'The statement to which you refer is ignorant nonsense. The doctrine of the Church of England about Holy Scripture is stated in her Sixth and Seventh. Articles, and that doctrine I most heartily accept."

This strikes us as a rather paltry evasion. The Sixth and Seventh Articles of the Church of England do not state the full Christian belief as to the Bible, but only the Protestant belief as against that of the Church of Rome. They emphasise two points, and two points only: first, that the Scriptures contain all that is necessary to salvation, so that no man is at the Pope's mercy for a seat in heaven; second, that fourteen books of the Roman Catholic Bible are apocryphal, and cannot be used to establish any doctrine. The general Christian view of the Bible, common to Catholics and Protestants, is taken for granted, as it had not then been brought into controversy. There is one word in the Sixth Article, however, which may be commended to Dr. Farrar's attention. The last clause explains what is meant by "Holy Scripture," and runs as follows:—"In the name of the holy Scripture we do understand those Canonical Books of the Old and New Testament, of whose authority was never any doubt in the Church." Now, unless Dr. Farrar means to juggle with the word "authority"—and we do not doubt his capacity for doing so—it is idle for him to say that he believes in the Bible according to these terms. He does *not* believe, for instance, in the "authority" of the book of Jonah; on the contrary, he believes that Jonah did not write it, and that it is not history, but romance, from beginning to end. If *this* is believing in the Bible, then Atheistic lecturers believe in it as well as Dr. Farrar. He does not believe that Jonah spent three days in a whale's belly—nor do they; he does not believe that Jonah's deep-sea adventure was a prefiguration of the burial of Jesus Christ—nor do they; he does not believe that the Jonah story is any the truer because Jesus Christ really or apparently believed it—nor do they; he simply believes that the story's moral is a good one, as far as it represents people who are not Jews as entitled to consideration—and so do they. Substantially there is not the smallest difference between them. The only discernible difference is a hypothetical one. Dr. Farrar claims that the book of Jonah is inspired. But he also claims that everything good and true—that is, everything worth reading—is inspired. "Very well then," the Atheist may reply, "I agree with you still, in substance. The only point in dispute between us is whether there is a God who interferes with the natural course of things, either in the external world or in the human mind. But on your definition of the word *inspired*, this makes no particular difference to any one book or collection of books. And unless you alter (and narrow) your theory of inspiration, our difference begins outside, not inside, the library—and is, in brief, not practical, but metaphysical."

But let us return to Dr. Farrar's method of proving his sufficient orthodoxy; and let us tell him that if he will only pursue it far enough, he may get rid of the Bible altogether.

Suppose we take Pearson's classic *Exposition of the Creed*, and open it at his address "to the Reader." In the second paragraph he writes as follows:—"The Creed, without controversy, is a brief comprehension of the objects of our Christian faith, and is generally taken to contain all things necessary to be believed." Now this Creed does not mention the Bible at all. A heathen might read it, and never infer from it that there was such a thing as the Scriptures in existence. What then is to prevent Dr. Farrar, or some more audacious clergyman, from saying that he does not believe in the Bible, as it is nowhere laid down as necessary to be believed; but that his orthodoxy is nevertheless unimpeachable, because he "most heartily accepts" the Catholic and Apostolic Creed which is "without controversy" an accurate compendium of the Christian faith, and which, being prescribed in the Prayer Book, is of course binding—and is *alone* binding—on every loyal son of the Church of England?

Dr. Farrar claims, as a clergyman, what he calls a "Christian liberty" in dealing with the Bible; although, if God has indeed spoken in the Bible, it is difficult to see what liberty a Christian can have but that of absolute belief and obedience. In a lengthy footnote of his volume which we have been criticising, he refers to the famous "Essays and Reviews Case," and the decisions of the judges in the Court of Arches and in the Privy Council. Dr. Lushington laid it down that: "Provided the Articles and Formularies are not contravened, the law lays down no limits of construction, no rule of interpretation, of the Scriptures." Lord Westbury declared that the Sixth Article of the Church of England was based upon "the revelations of the Holy Spirit," and therefore the Bible might be denominated "holy" and be said to be "the Word of God"; but this was not "distinctly predicated of every statement and representation contained in every part of the Old and New Testaments." "The framers of the Articles," Lord Westbury added,

59

"have not used the word 'inspiration' as applied to the Holy Scriptures, nor have they laid down anything as to the nature, extent, or limits of that operation of the Holy Spirit."

According to this sapient judgment, which perhaps is very good law, and covers all possible developments of the Higher Criticism, every member of the Church of England is bound to regard the Bible as containing "the revelations of the Holy Spirit," but is not bound to regard it as a work of "inspiration." A judge, with his legal spectacles on, is notoriously able to discriminate subtleties where laymen see only what is plain; and clergymen may take advantage of his preternatural sagacity, without being able in the long run to impose upon the common sense of the people, who will always look upon "revelation" and "inspiration" as interchangeable terms.

It is quite natural that Dr. Farrar should wish to get rid of this word "inspiration," since it can no longer be defined without danger. But we must remind him that, if it does not occur in the Church Articles, it certainly does occur in the Bible. "All scripture," Paul said, "is given by inspiration of God." [12]

And as the New Testament was not then in existence, Paul of course referred to the Old Testament. This was the "holy scriptures" which Timothy had "known from a child." And Peter is, if possible, more definite than Paul. He speaks of the "more sure word of prophecy," surer than the very voice heard by the three disciples on the mount of transfiguration. This "prophecy of the scripture" he declares to be never of "any private interpretation"—which means, according to the commentators, that it did not spring from any knowledge or personal conjecture in the prophet. Finally, he clinches his exposition by affirming that "holy men of God spake as they were moved by the Holy Ghost." [13]

According to the Sixth Article of the Church of England, both these epistles, bearing the names of Paul and Peter, are among the

---

[12] Timothy iii. 16.

[13] 2 Peter i. 19-21. We quote this epistle as Peter's, because it passes as his in the New Testament, not because it was really his writing.

60

books "of whose authority was never any doubt in the Church." Dr. Farrar is therefore bound by them in logic and honor. He is not free to cast aside the Biblical term of *inspiration* nor free to minimise as he pleases the "moving" influence of the Holy Ghost in either the New or the Old Testament. As a clergyman of the Church of England, he assumes an unwarrantable freedom; a freedom which is no more sanctioned by her Articles than it is by the letter or spirit of the Scriptures. He departs entirely from the primitive and real position of Protestantism; namely, that the Bible is the absolute standard of faith and practice, and that, wherever it is dark or dubious, it must be interpreted by itself. He treads the *via media* of compromise and irrationality; neither going over to Rome, which claims to be inspired, like the Bible, and to be the vehicle of the living voice of God for the infallible interpretation of the written revelation—nor going over to Rationalism, which regards the Catholic Church as but a human institution, and the Bible as but a human composition. Believe that God has spoken, according to the words of Paul and Peter, and the Catholic theory is the only satisfactory one; disbelieve it, and there is no logical alternative but the most thoroughgoing Rationalism.

XI. AN ORIENTAL BOOK

Dr. Farrar stumbles, on one occasion, against the true theory of the Bible. Having to furnish an excuse, if not a justification, for the outrageous crudity of a good deal of its language, he reminds us that decorum changes with time and place. "The rigid external modesty and propriety of modern and English literature," he observes, "is disgusted and offended by statements which gave no such shock to ancient and Eastern readers." And he adds that "The plain-spokenness of Orientals involved no necessary offence against abstract morality." This is true enough, but the argument should be developed. What is urged in extenuation of the grossness of the Scripture is really applicable all round—to its mythology, its legends, its religion, its philosophy, its ethics, and its poetry. The Bible is an oriental book. And this one statement, when properly understood, gives us the true key to its interpretation, the real criterion of its character, and the just measure of its value.

It has been well remarked that the ordinary Christian in this part of the world appears to imagine that the Bible dropped down from heaven—in English. Even the expounders of the Higher Criticism, in our own country, read it first in their mother tongue; and although they afterwards read it in the original Greek, and sometimes in the original Hebrew, they are under the witchery of early impressions, and their apologetics are almost entirely founded upon the vernacular Bible. Thus they lose sight, and their readers never catch a glimpse, of the predominant element, the governing factor, of the problem.

All the Bibles in the world, like all the religions in the world, came from the East. "Not one of them," as Max Müller remarks, "has been conceived, composed, or written down in Europe." [14]

---

[14] Max Müller, Natural Religion, p. 538.

He classes the *Pilgrim's Progress* among the "many books which have exercised a far greater influence on religious faith and moral conduct than the Bibles of the world"; but Bunyan's originality was artistic and not religious; he absorbed the Puritanism of his age, and reproduced it in the form of a magnificent allegory. Religious originality does not belong to the Western mind, which is too scientific and practical. Every one of the fashionable crazes that spring up from time to time, and have their day and give place to a successor, is merely a garment from the old wardrobe of superstition. This is true of Theosophy, for instance; all its doctrines, ideas, and jargon being borrowed from India. "There are five countries only," Max Müller says, "which have been the birthplace of Sacred Books: (1) India, (2) Persia, (3) China, (4) Palestine, (5) Arabia." All come from the East, and all have a generic and historic resemblance. Not one of them was written by the founder of its religion. Moses did not write the Pentateuch, Christ did not write a line of the New Testament, Mohammed did not write the Koran, Zoroaster did not write the Avesta, the Buddhist Scriptures were not written by Buddha, and the Vedic hymns are far more ancient than writing in India. All these Sacred Books embody the accepted beliefs of whole peoples; all of them are canonical and authoritative; all contain very much the same ethical groundwork, in the form of elementary moral prohibitions; all of them are held to be of divine character; all of them become a kind of fetish, which is worshipped and obeyed at the expense of the free spirit of man, who is told not to be wise above what is written. Ecclesiastical or kingly authority has generally given these books their final form and character. Their establishment takes place in open daylight, but their origin is more or less shrouded in mystery. "It is curious," Max Müller says, "that wherever we have sacred books, they represent to us the oldest language of the country. It is so in India, it is the same in Persia, in China, in Palestine, and very nearly so in Arabia." [15] According to Max Müller, the Veda was referred to in India fifteen hundred years before Christ.

---

[15] *Natural Religion*, p. 295.

Consequently it precedes by many centuries even the earliest parts of the Bible:—

"The Vedic hymns come to us as a collection of sacred poetry, belonging to certain ancient families, and afterwards united in one collection, called the Rig-veda-samhitâ. The names of the poets, handed down by tradition, are in most cases purely imaginary names. What is really important is that in the hymns themselves the poets speak of their thoughts and words as *God-given*—this we can understand—while at a later time the theory came in that not the thoughts and words only, but every syllable, every letter, every accent, had been communicated to half-divine and half-human prophets by Brahma, so that the slightest mistake in pronunciation, even to the pronunciation of an accent, would destroy the charm and efficacy of these ancient prayers." [16]

With a slight variation of language, to suit the special circumstances, nearly all this would apply to the Bible.

Christianity, like Brahmanism, like Buddhism, like Mohammedanism, is a book religion. It is "God-given," or revealed, and its Bible has been elevated to a position of infallibility, above the reach of human reason, precisely like the Bibles of other oriental faiths. This sanctification of every thought and word and letter is declared by Max Müller to have been "the death-blow given to the Vedic religion," destroying its power of growth and change. A similar observation is made by Sir William Muir respecting the petrified gospel of the Koran:—

"From the stiff and rigid shroud in which it is thus swathed, the religion of Mohammed cannot emerge. It has no plastic power beyond that exercised in its earliest days. Hardened now and inelastic, it can neither adapt itself nor yet shape its votaries, nor even suffer them to shape themselves, to the varying circumstances, the wants and developments of mankind." [17]

---

[16] Max Müller, ibid, p. 558.
[17] Sir William Muir, Rise and Decline of Islam, pp. 40, 41.

64

How curious it is, after reading this strong passage, to come across a diametrically opposite one in the work of another eminent writer on the same subject. Professor Arnold closes his important book on the propagation of the Muslim faith with a reference to "the power of this religion to adapt itself to the peculiar characteristics and the stage of development of the people whose allegiance it seeks to win." [18] Historically, it is perfectly certain that Mohammedanism *has* been found compatible with a high degree of civilisation. Many instances might be given, but a single one is sufficient. The Mohammedan civilisation in Spain was far superior to the Christian civilisation which, after terrible bloodshed and enormous destruction, was established upon its ruins. The truth is, that religions always change when they must change, and never otherwise. When the necessity arises, learned divines will always be found to make the requisite accommodations. This, indeed, is the explanation of the labors of Dr. Farrar and other exponents of the Higher Criticism. They are simply accommodating Christianity, and the Bible with it, to the serious changes that have taken place in educated opinion and sentiment, in consequence of the development of physical science, the progress of historical criticism, and the growth of moral culture. All the truth in Sir William Muir's impeachment of Mohammedanism is no less applicable to Christianity. The Bible, like the Koran, and like every other revelation, stereotyped old ideas, and gave them a factitious longevity. Dr. Farrar himself not only admits, but contends, that the Bible has been invoked against every advance in science, politics, and sociology. What more could be said of the Koran or any other sacred book?

Bring any oriental religion into Europe, and it must change or perish. Christianity is not true, as Mr. Gladstone and so many orthodox apologists have argued, because the Christian nations are at the top of civilisation. The Caucasian mind led the world before the advent of Christianity, and it is doing the same now. Christians

---

[18] T. W. Arnold, The Preaching of Islam.

are apt to forget that Greece and Italy are in Europe, and that Athens and Rome—two imperishable names in the world's history—were far-shining cities before a good deal of the Old Testament was written.

Keep any oriental religion in the East, however, and there is no saying how long it will last unaltered. Do not travellers talk of the unchanging East? The civilisation of China is almost what it was thousands of years ago. Syrian life to-day is like a picture from the Bible. And the old Orient, as Flaubert said, is the land of religions; and where Asia looks upon Europe, and the communication between them began of yore, you may sample all the faiths of antiquity. Flaubert remarked that the assemblage of all the old religions in Syria was something incredible; it was enough to study for centuries. [19]

Asia spawned forth all the great religions, and produced all the great revelations. Arabia is in Africa, but the Arabs are not Africans; they belong to the Semitic race, like the Jews, and the Koran embodies Jewish and other Semitic traditions.

The Bible, then, is an oriental book, an Asiatic book, in spite of the Greek elements which are incorporated in the New Testament, notably in the fourth Gospel. It has never been in harmony with the real life of the West. When it has dominated the life of a particular locality, for a certain period, the result has been something typically non-European; as in the case of Scotland under the despotism of the Kirk, whose spiritual slaves prompted Heine's epigram that the Presbyterian Scotchman was a Jew, born in the north, who ate pork. Modern civilisation is mainly a return to the spirit of secular progress which inspired the immortal achievements of Greece and Rome.

"The revival of learning and the Renaissance are memorable as the first sturdy breasting by humanity of the hither slope of the great hollow which lies between us and the ancient world. The

---

[19] Flaubert, Correspondence, vol. i., p. 344.

modern man, reformed and regenerated by knowledge, looks across it, and recognises on the opposite ridge, in the far-shining cities and stately porticoes, in the art, politics, and science of antiquity, many more ties of kinship and sympathy than in the mighty concave between, wherein dwell his Christian ancestry, in the dim light of scholasticism and theology." [20]

Well, if we once fully recognise the Bible as an oriental book, we are on the road to its complete comprehension. Its grossness of speech, its gratuitous reference to animal functions, its designation of males by their sexual attributes even on the most serious occasions, its religious observances in connection with pregnancy and birth, its very rite of circumcision; all this, and much more, becomes perfectly intelligible. It is in keeping with all we know of the ideas, practices, and language of the East. Moreover, we perceive why it is that similarities to the theology, the poetry, and the ethics of the Bible have been so liberally disclosed by the progress of oriental studies. The Bible, being brought from the East, has to be carried back there to be properly understood. It is true that Christian divines have offered their own explanation of these similarities. At first they declared them to be Satanic anticipations, devilish pre-mockeries, of God's own truth. Then they declared them to be confused echoes of the oracles of Jehovah. Finally, they declare them to be evidences of the fact that, although God chose the Jewish race as the medium of his special revelation, he also revealed himself partially to other nations. But these explanations are alike fantastic. They rest upon no ground of history or evolution. The real explanation is that the Bible is one of the many sacred books of the East. Its differences from the rest are not of kind, but of degree; and any superiority that may be claimed for it must henceforth be argued upon this basis.

This oriental Bible is at utter variance with the vital beliefs, the political and social tendencies, and the ethical aspirations, of the present age. Science has destroyed its naive supernaturalism;

---

[20] James Cotter Morison, The Service of Man, p. 178.

reason has placed its personal God—the magnified, non-natural man—in his own niche in the world's Pantheon; philosophy has carried us far beyond its primitive conceptions of human society; our morality has outgrown its hardness and insularity, however we may still appreciate its finer ejaculations; even the most pious Christians, with the exception of a few "peculiar" people, only pay a hypocritical homage to its clearest injunctions; and the higher development of decency and propriety makes us turn from its crude expressions with a growing sense of disgust, while the progress of humanity fills us more and more with a loathing of its frightful wars and ruthless massacres, its tales of barbaric cruelty, and its crowning infamy of an everlasting hell.

XII. FICTITIOUS SUPREMACY

There are two remarkable characteristics of present-day apologies for Christianity: one is extravagant laudation of Jesus as man and teacher, the other is extravagant laudation of the Bible as ethics and literature. Both these characteristics are really signs of the decadence of positive faith. Anyone who sincerely believed in the deity of Jesus would shrink from praising his human virtues. To such a person it would savor strongly of impertinence. Nor would anyone who really believed the Bible to be the Word of God make it the subject of meaner panegyrics. It seems ridiculous to argue that God wrote with unusual power and sublimity, and is actually the very first of known authors. But this is what Dr. Farrar does, essentially, in the last six chapters of his volume. No wonder, therefore, that all the vices of his style are displayed in the accomplishment of this extraordinary task. He has to make several quotations from great or distinguished writers, but he catches no literary infection from them. One of these quotations is from brave old George Fox. "I saw," the great Quaker wrote, "that there was an ocean of darkness and death; but an infinite ocean of Light and Love flowed over the ocean of Darkness; and in that I saw the infinite love of God." This is magnificent writing. It has vision, force, and simplicity. In its way it could hardly be beaten. And how poor in comparison is the turgid pulpit rhetoric of Dr. Farrar!

We are told by this wordy defender of the faith that the Christian Scriptures are "the Supreme Bible of Humanity"—as though, if it be the Word of God, it could be anything less. Our attention is called to its "unique transcendence"—which is a penny-a-lining pleonasm. We are informed that it has "triumphed with ease over the assaults of its enemies"—which is a remarkably modest assertion, especially in view of the fact that the "enemies" of the Bible were, for fifteen hundred years, generally subdued by persecution, imprisonment, torture, assassination, and the burning of their writings. We are further informed that the Bible commands the reverence, guides the thoughts, educates the souls, and kindles the moral aspirations of men "through all the world"—which is an extremely sober statement in view of the fact that all the *nominal* Christians, not to be too precise about the *real* ones, do not amount to more than a fourth of the world's inhabitants. So wonderful a book is the Bible that "the Lord Jesus Christ himself did not disdain to quote from the Old Testament"—which was his own word, in the sense that it was (professedly) written under divine inspiration. This is absurd enough, but it is nothing to the rapturous eulogy of the Bible which follows it. "All the best and brightest English verse [not *some*, mark, but *all!*], from the poems of Chaucer to the plays of Shakespeare in their noblest parts, are echoes of its lessons; and from Cowper to Wordsworth," Dr. Farrar says, "from Coleridge to Tennyson, the greatest of our poets have drawn from its pages their loftiest wisdom." Really, one is tempted to ask whether such stuff as this is possible in any other country than England, or perhaps America; and whether, even in England or America, it is possible outside churches, chapels, and Sunday-schools. Sixty pages later—Dr. Farrar could not sober down in that long interval—he declares that "It was the Bible which created the prose literature of England." Now if this were true it would not serve Dr. Farrar's ostensible purpose. It would not prove that the Bible is a divine revelation. It would only prove the historical—that is to say, the largely accidental—importance of the Authorised Version of the Bible in the development of English literature. But this declaration of Dr. Farrar's is *not* true. The Authorised Version did not initiate, it rather closed, a period of our literary history. The English of the translators in their Preface is vastly different from the English of their translation. Indeed, they were rather collators than translators. They took the older versions as the basis of their work, they altered as little as possible, and the alterations they did make were strictly in harmony with the time-honored style of those older versions, a style which was even then very archaic. Dr. Marsh, himself a devout Christian, contends that "the dialect of this translation was

70

not, at the time of the revision, or, indeed, at any other period, the actual current book-language nor the colloquial speech of the English people." He maintains that it was "a consecrated diction" which had been "gradually built up" from the time of Wycliffe. [21] Its language was not the language of Chaucer's prose, nor even of Wycliffe's own prose, any more than it was the language of Bacon's or Shakespeare's, or even that of divines like Hooker. The Authorised Version is indeed a monument of English, but of special English. It has always stood aside from the main development of English prose. Of course it has exercised a considerable influence, but that influence has been chiefly indirect. From the young naive prose of Malory to the mature and calculated prose of Swift—not to come farther—there is a clear stream of development, to which the language and style of the English Bible have contributed infinitely less than is generally assumed. With the single exception of Bunyan's masterpiece, which stands apart and alone, it is difficult to name a first-class prose competition that was greatly indebted to our Authorised Version. Even the divines disregarded it as a literary model, and perhaps most conspicuously so in the seventeenth century, immediately after its publication.

Dr. Farrar is entirely wrong in declaring that the Bible created the prose literature of England. Even if he only means that English prose was vastly profited by the religious literature which followed upon the heels of the Reformation, it is easy to reply that this literature was mainly controversial and never remarkable for the higher graces and dexterities. For those virtues, prior to the time of Taylor and South, we must turn to secular and even to "profane" compositions; a fact which is well known to every real student of English literature.

The next device of Dr. Farrar's advocacy would be astounding if one did not know the muddle-headed public for whom he writes. He devotes a monstrous number of pages to the citing of a "cloud of witnesses to the glory and supremacy of the Holy Scriptures,"

---

[21] George P. Marsh, Lectures on the English Language (Murray), pp. 441, 445.

71

beginning with the great John Henry Newman and winding up with the notorious Hall Caine. Sandwiched between these dissimilar "witnesses" are Heine, Goethe, Rousseau, Wesley, Emerson, Carlyle, Huxley, Arnold, Ruskin, and a host of others. Most of them were Christians, and afford a partisan testimony which is not very valuable. In any case, there is no real argument in a list of names. When a man is being tried on a definite charge, it is idle to recite a catalogue of his distinguished friends. Witnesses to character are only heard in mitigation of sentence after the jury has returned a verdict of Guilty. Perhaps this fact had its influence on Dr. Farrar's mind; at any rate, he calls his "cloud of witnesses" when he has ended all he had to say in the form of argument.

These witnesses, moreover, are jumbled together without the slightest discrimination. Let us take a few illustrations to show the futility of Dr. Farrar's method.

John Wesley cried "Give me the book of God! Here is knowledge enough for me. Let me be a man of one book." Yes, and John Wesley believed in witchcraft, and honestly declared that to throw over witchcraft was to throw over the Bible. He had, also, his own way of proving "the divine inspiration of the Holy Scriptures." He wrote a "Clear and Concise Demonstration," from which we take the following extract:—

"I beg leave to propose a short, clear, and strong argument to prove the divine inspiration of the Holy Scriptures.

"The Bible must be the invention either of good men or angels, bad men or devils, or of God.

"(1) It could not be the invention of good men or angels; for they neither would nor could make a book, and tell lies all the time they were writing it, saying, 'Thus saith the Lord,' when it was their own invention.

"(2) It could not be the invention of bad men or devils; for they would not make a book which commands all duty, forbids all sin, and condemns their souls to hell to all eternity.

72

"(3) Therefore, I draw this conclusion, that the Bible must be given by divine inspiration." [22]

Could anything be more childish than this ridiculous play upon the word "invention," and this absurd supposition that "good men" and "bad men" are two sharp divisions of the human species? We know that all men are mixtures, and that honest men may be mistaken, and tell falsehoods without lying. We are therefore able to measure the value of John Wesley's "demonstration" that the Bible is inspired.

John Ruskin thanks his mother for daily reading the Bible with him in his childhood, and daily making him learn a part of it by heart. This is seized upon by Dr. Farrar, who places it in his list of testimonies. But it might have been wise—it would certainly have been honest—to tell the reader how Ruskin views the Bible. This great writer has formulated four theories of the Bible, the third of which he has declared to be "for the last half-century the theory of the soundest scholars and thinkers in Europe." And what is this theory? Here it is in Ruskin's own words:—

"That the mass of religious Scripture contains merely the best efforts which we hitherto know to have been made by any of the races of men towards the discovery of some relations with the spiritual world; that they are only trustworthy as expressions of the enthusiastic visions or beliefs of earnest men oppressed by the world's darkness, and have no more authoritative claim on our faith than the religious speculations and histories of the Egyptians, Greeks, Persians, and Indians; but are, in common with all these, to be reverently studied, as containing a portion, divinely appointed, of the best wisdom which the human intellect, earnestly seeking for help from God, has hitherto been able to gather between birth and death." [23]

---

[22] John Wesley's Works (1865), vol. xi., pp. 464-465.
[23] Time and Tide, pp. 48, 49. It should be noted that the Letters in this pregnant little volume were written by Ruskin as far back as 1867.

Surely this is a very different view of the Bible from the one which is presented by Dr. Farrar. Setting aside a little religious phraseology, a Freethinker might endorse Ruskin's theory of the Bible. Everything is substantially granted to the Freethinker when it is admitted that the Bible has "no authoritative claim on our faith." Whatever truth and beauty it contains may then be thankfully accepted.

Professor Huxley's famous eulogy of the Bible, as a book to be read in Board Schools, is made the most of by Dr. Farrar. He must have winced, however, at Huxley's reference to what a sensible teacher would "eliminate" as "not desirable for children to occupy themselves with." He was not sensitive enough to wince at the statement that "even the noble Stoic, Marcus Antoninus, is too high and refined for an ordinary child"—which is virtually a testimonial in his favor for grown-up men and women. Dr. Farrar crows lustily over what he calls "Professor Huxley's testimony to the unique glory of the Scriptures." It is perhaps well for him that Huxley is incapable of resenting this misrepresentation. Still, it must be admitted that on this occasion, as on one or two others, Huxley did gratuitously play into the hands of the enemy. He might have known the kind of use they would make of his "graceful concessions."

Dr. Farrar had not the honesty to tell his readers that Huxley had the most sovereign contempt for *his* theory of the Bible. The great Agnostic held, for instance, that "belief in a demonic world" is inculcated throughout the New Testament, and that this belief is "totally devoid of foundation." He declared that Inspiration, in the school of the Higher Criticism, is "deprived of its old intelligible sense," and is "watered down into a mystification." He laughed at the miracles of the Gospels, and made great fun of the story of the bedevilled Gadarean swine. He held that religion and morality have really no necessary connection, and sneered at the "supernaturalists"—gentlemen like Dr. Farrar—who took to patronising morality when they saw its importance, and "have ever since tried to persuade mankind that the existence of ethics is bound up with that of supernaturalism." [24]

To accept a testimonial from such a writer is abject on the part of a clergyman defending the inspiration of the Bible; and to parade it is simply contemptible. More than fifty years ago, when this petty trick of Christian apologetics was coming into vogue, it was rebuked by Newman, who disdained as "unworthy" the practice of "boasting of the admissions of infidels concerning the beauty or utility of the Christian system, as though," he added with fine sarcasm, "it were a great thing for a divine gift to obtain praise for human excellence." [25]

Dr. Farrar's citation of Matthew Arnold is open to the same kind of criticism. "He retained but little faith in the miraculous," we are told, and "his creed was anything but orthodox." But is it fair to suggest that Arnold had any creed at all? He rejected the idea of a personal God, he regarded Jesus as a merely human teacher, and it is evident from his books and his published correspondence that he had no belief in personal immortality. As for his "faith in the miraculous," it was not "little," with or without the "but"; it was a minus quantity. He positively disbelieved in the miraculous. It was a part of his plain message to the Churches that the reign of the Bible miracles was doomed, that they were all fairy tales, and that, if the fate of the Bible was bound up with theirs, the Bible was doomed too. Arnold said all this when he was living, and it is useless for Dr. Farrar to disguise the fact, or to minimise it by artful phrases. We commend to his attention—would that we could commend it to the attention of his readers!—the following passage from a letter of Arnold's to Sir Mountstuart Grant Duff, dated July 22, 1882:—

"The central fact of the situation always remains to me this: that whereas the basis of things amidst all chance and change has even in Europe generally been for ever so long supernatural Christianity,

---

[24] Huxley, Science and Christian Tradition, pp. xv., 25, 54, etc.
[25] John Henry Newman, University Sermons, p. 71.

and far more so in England than in Europe generally, this basis is certainly going—going amidst the full consciousness of the continentals that it is going, and amidst the provincial unconsciousness of the English that it is going." [26]

Considering what Arnold's views really were, is it of any use to make the statement of rather doubtful accuracy that the Bible was his "chief and constant study"? Is it not misleading to talk of his "intense reverence and admiration for the Sacred Books"? He did not regard them as *sacred*. He studied and valued the Bible as literature, not as revelation; and it is monstrous to cite him as a witness in favor of the Bible as it is represented in the school of Dr. Farrar.

We need not waste time over Dr. Farrar's *banal* remark that Livingstone, Stanley, and the Bible together have caused "the extension of the British protectorate over 170,000 square miles" in a certain part of Africa. We may treat with the same indifference his boast of the millions of copies of the "Sacred Books" distributed by the British and American Bible Societies. Such "evidences" are only fit for the street-corner. Only a low-minded, commercial-sodden Christian could imagine that the multiplication of copies of a book is any sort of testimony to its intrinsic truth and value; and in this particular case the demand is a forced one, depending on the incessant stimulus of the supply.

Another argument of Dr. Farrar's for the "supremacy" of the Bible is based upon the history of Christian martyrdoms. He gives several instances of Christians, old and young, rich and poor, high-placed and humble, who have died for their faith, and entered "the dark river and its still waters with a smile upon their faces." He attributes their fortitude to trust in the promises of the Bible. But he does not tell us how it proves the truth of the Bible either as history or as revelation. Millions of Jews have died at the hands of Christian bigots, and their heroism amidst torture and massacre has never been exceeded in human annals. Does this prove that the

---

[26] Matthew Arnold, Letters, vol. ii., p. 201.

New Testament is not a revelation, and that Jesus Christ was not God? Men of other faiths have faced death with sublime courage. Does this prove that their beliefs were accurate? Mohammedans are notoriously ready to die for their religion; the Mohammedan dervishes in the Soudan never quailed before the most murderous storm of shell and bullets; they fell in thousands at Omdurman, and the Khalifa's standard-bearer, when all around him were slain, stood upright under the holy flag, with a smile of defiance on his face, which never left it until he sank shot-riddled upon the heap of his dead comrades. Does this prove that the Koran is the Word of God?

The orthodox argument seems to be this: if a Christian dies for the Bible, that proves it to be a divine book; if a devotee of any other faith dies for his Sacred Scripture. That proves nothing—unless it be the obstinacy of wrong opinions.

There is something intensely comical in the seriousness with which Dr. Farrar relates the martyrdom of Christians who were put to death by other Christians. He does not see that all he gains on one side is lost on the other, that Christian persecution balances Christian fortitude, and that nothing is left to the credit of his account. He devotes a whole page to the murder of Margaret Lachlan and Margaret Wilson by "brutal and tyrannous bigots" at Wigton in 1677. These two women were Covenanting Christians, and their murderers were Episcopalian Christians. They died singing psalms which their murderers believed to be the word of God. It is difficult to see what advantage the Bible derives from this incident.

One may be interested by the reminder that Oliver Cromwell quoted two verses from the hundred and seventeenth Psalm after his victory at Dunbar; but one may remember on one's own account that David Leslie, the defeated Scots general, was as devout a Christian and Bible-reader as Oliver Cromwell, and that his piety was stimulated by the presence in his camp of a whole congregation of Presbyterian ministers. Altogether it is a pity that

Dr. Farrar picks his illustrations in this one-eyed fashion. He forgets that other people may have two eyes, and see on both sides of them. He almost invites the sarcasm that the one-eyed man is only a leader amongst the blind.

The real secret of whatever supremacy belongs to the Bible is to be sought in a different direction. It was long ago remarked by a French Freethinker, in a work attributed to Boulanger, but really written by D'Holbach, that education and authority were the two great pillars of the Christian revelation.

"If a body of men in possession of power, and able to like advantage of the credulity of mankind, were to find their interest concerned in doing so, they would make men believe at the end of a few centuries that the adventures of Don Quixote are perfectly true, and that the prophecies of Nostrodamus have been inspired by God himself. By dint of glosses, of commentaries, and of allegories, it is easy to discover and to prove what one pleases; however glaring an imposture may be, it can be made at last, by the aid of time, cunning, and power, to pass for truth which no one must doubt. Deceivers who are obstinate, and who are supported by public authority, can make ignorant people, who are always credulous, believe anything, especially if they can persuade them that there is merit in not noticing inconsistencies, contradictions, and palpable absurdities, and that there is danger in making use of their reason."[27]

Abolish all the Churches that exist for the purpose of preaching up the Bible as a divine revelation; destroy all the clerical corporations that live and operate upon this basis; take away, at least, the public revenues and special privileges they enjoy; deprive them of the patronage of the legislature and the government; remove their Holy Scriptures from the public schools, where they are retained in defiance of the principles of civil and religious liberty; let little children no longer be suborned in favor of the supernatural claims of this book before they are able to judge for

---

[27] Examen Critique de St. Paul, c. 3.

78

themselves; let the Bible take its own chance with the rest of the world's literature; and then, and not till then, can its natural supremacy be established. But the clergy know that such an experiment would be absolutely fatal to their pretensions. They dare not accept a fair field and no favor. They know in their heart of hearts that they are serving a lie. Their dishonesty is apparent at every turn. Dr. Farrar calls upon England to "cling to her open Bible." Well, the Peculiar People do so. They read the open Bible, they follow its teaching as closely as possible, they obey the commandments of Jesus Christ. And what is the result? They are cast into prison like felons. One of them is suffering that pain and indignity at the present moment.

A good husband, a good father, a good neighbor, a good citizen, he has committed the crime of practically believing what Dr. Farrar and the rest of the clergy facetiously preach—namely, that the Bible is the Book of God, and the divine rule of faith and conduct. For this crime he is imprisoned under the verdict of a Christian jury and the sentence of a Christian judge; and not a single Christian minister raises his voice against this infamous spectacle. Christianity is now only an organised hypocrisy. It subsists upon an inherited fund of power, wealth, and reputation. Even the clergy have no vital belief in the inspiration of the Bible. It is merely the charter under which they trade. It is a source of oracular texts for their ambiguous sermons. It is lauded and adored, and neglected and defied. To bring it into disbelief and contempt by argument and ridicule is a misdemeanor; to bring it into disbelief and contempt by acting upon it is a felony. The only safe course is that adopted by the clergy, who neither believe it nor disbelieve it, but use it as it serves their occasions; and as long as it answers their ends it will remain the Book of God.

Let us not be misunderstood. We are far from desiring to engage in a crusade against the Bible as a collection of ancient literature. We are neither called upon nor disposed to deny its real merits, however they are exaggerated in religious circles. It undoubtedly contains some fine poetry, occasional pathos, and more frequent sublimity. Its style has nearly always the charm of simplicity. All this may be allowed without playing into the hands of the super-naturalists. Further than this we need not go. In our opinion, it is absurd to place the Bible at the top of human compositions. More than sixty writers are alleged to have contributed to its production, but the whole mass of them do not rival the magnificent and fecund genius of Shakespeare. Above all, they have no wit or humour, in which Shakespeare abounds; and wit and humor belong to the higher development of intellect and emotion. No, the Bible is not the unapproachable masterpiece which it is declared to be by its fanatical devotees. But whatever its intrinsic merits may prove to be, in the light of long and free appreciation, the Bible cannot be accepted as a revelation from God without wilful self-delusion on the part of educated men and women. If God had a message for his children, he would at least make it clear; but this revelation needs another revelation to explain it, and creeds and commentaries are the symbols of its obscurity. God's message would tell us what we could not otherwise learn, but there is no such information in the Bible. God would apprise us of what he specially desired us to remember, and would not mix it confusedly with a tremendous mass of alien matter. God would not puzzle us; he would enlighten us. He would make his communication so clear that a wayfaring man, though a fool, could understand it; whereas, if the Bible be his communication, no wayfaring man, unless he *is* a fool, pretends to understand it. God would not clog his message with myths, legends, mysteries, absurdities, falsehoods, and filth; and leave us to extricate it with endless labor and perpetual uncertainty. The so-called Higher Criticism is therefore as absurd as the old Orthodoxy in calling the Bible a work of inspiration. Its exponents affirm that God has left us to our own knowledge and reason in regard to every other subject but religion and morality. They are Evolutionists in part. But the principle of Evolution must be applied over the whole field. Everything is natural, and happens under the universal law of causation. There are no miracles, and there never were any except in ignorant imaginations. But the death of miracles is the death of inspiration. The triumph of science involves the ruin of every supernatural system. Revelation is necessarily miraculous, and when the belief in miracles expires the death-knell rings for every Book of God. We are then left to the discipline of culture.

And what is culture? It is steeping our minds in the wisest and loveliest thoughts of all the ages. And each of us may thus make his own Bible for himself—a true Bible of Humanity.

www.ingramcontent.com/pod-product-compliance
Lightning Source LLC
Chambersburg PA
CBHW011801040426
42448CB00017B/3327